**University
for the
Creative Arts**

Fort Pitt
Rochester
Kent
ME1 1DZ

Tel: 01634 888734

E-mail:
gatewayrochester@uca.ac.uk

Tie-dye

Tie-dye

designs
materials
technique

Sara Néa

 VAN NOSTRAND REINHOLD COMPANY

New York   Cincinnati   Toronto   London   Melbourne

This book was originally published
in Swedish under the title
Knytbatik by I. C. A. Förlaget.
Västeras, Sweden

Copyright © Sara Néa and
I. C. A. Förlaget, Västeras 1969
English translation © Van Nostrand
Reinhold Company Ltd. 1971

Library of Congress Catalog Card
Number 73–156129
ISBN 0 442 05943 4 cl.
ISBN 0 442 05944 2 pb.

Photography—Johan Pihlgren,
Studio Johan, Göteborg
Fredrik Lundgren, Fredriks Foto,
Västeras
Nils Magner, Motiv-Foto, Göteborg

This book is set in Univers and is
printed and bound in Great Britain
by Jarrold & Sons Ltd, Norwich

Published by Van Nostrand
Reinhold Company
450 West 33rd St, New York,
N.Y. 10001
and Van Nostrand Reinhold
Company Ltd
Windsor House, 46 Victoria Street,
London S.W.1

Published simultaneously in Canada
by Van Nostrand Reinhold
Company Ltd

Contents

Introduction

The craft of tie-dye, or tie and dye, is one of the oldest in the world for making colored designs on fabric. Its origins are unknown, but first records of the craft date back to the sixth century AD and are to be found in the East—in particular in China, India, Japan and Indonesia. The craft was also practised by the Incas of Peru before the Spanish conquest in the fifteenth century and is still practised today in various parts of South America, also in Africa. Europe has only recently discovered the creative possibilities of tie and dye, although early evidence of the craft is to be found in Slav and Scandinavian countries.

The technique of tie and dye is, simply, to isolate parts of the fabric and dye the rest. Originally, wax was much used to isolate the undyed parts. This process of resist dyeing with wax is more correctly known as "batik" work. Tie and dye, as the name suggests, actually involves tying before dyeing. The process involves three equally important stages: folding, isolating (by tying), and dyeing. The first stage varies according to the shape of the design required. For example, for a striped effect the material is usually folded or gathered horizontally; for circular patterns the material is rolled up rather like an umbrella. The second stage involves tying string or thread tightly around the material wherever it is to be kept free of dye. The material is finally immersed in a dye bath. The result is the soft and living play of color characteristic of this form of textile design.

What to tie-dye

Clothes are an obvious choice, particularly leisure clothes which can allow more scope for the imagination. Jackets and shirts are popular, also simple skirts, dresses, trousers and aprons. Mother and daughter or big and little sister designs are fun to make using broadly similar patterns but scaling the size down to fit the smaller models.

If you do not wish to tie-dye on a large scale you can use the technique to liven up scarfs, pockets, collars and borders. Matching shawls and handbags are another possibility, as are hats and caps to go with dresses.

It is tempting to buy a plain ready-made dress with the idea of tie-dyeing it. This can work if the dress is simple, but on the whole it is rather difficult to tie-dye a ready-made garment. On the other hand it is often a good idea to cut out a garment and tack it together before dyeing the individual pieces separately.

The beginner should experiment with straightforward projects such as cushion-covers or table-runners, both of which are eminently suitable for tie-dye work. Everyday articles such as waste-paper baskets, boxes and telephone-directories can be

"Flower vision."
Spontaneous tie-dye design.

covered in tie-dyed material and given a foam-rubber backing. They brighten the home—and also make most acceptable gifts.

A well-executed piece of tie-dye work can make a beautiful wall decoration or "picture." Stretch the material over a frame and illuminate it from behind to bring out the full beauty of the design. Practically all tie-dyed work is seen at its best if a degree of transparency is obtained. Thus many professional tie-dye craftsmen use their work for window decoration, displaying pieces small enough to fit inside the window-pane. Such display work is usually executed in fine batiste and stretched over a wire frame. It is sometimes decorated with a scalloped edging of glass or wooden beads.

Which fabrics to use

First and foremost the material you choose should be color-fast so that you can wash your handiwork in an ordinary machine wash. For this you need color-fast dyes—and these will only work on natural fiber materials such as cotton, linen, poplin, canvas and silk. Non-iron or minimum-iron materials are unsuitable because they have been subjected to a glazing process which prevents the dye from penetrating properly into the fibers. The glaze can never be entirely removed, even if the material is boiled and reboiled. Do not use cotton mixtures containing wool, nylon and synthetic fibers.

The best materials are undoubtedly finely woven cotton and batiste, because the dye penetrates into them easily and the pattern is more finely etched. Batiste is good for all fine work. Fine materials are also easier to handle in the dye bath, and the container used for the dye can be smaller and the quantity of dye reduced. The choice, however, is not limited to the cotton family. Piqué and similar raised materials can be used for special effects, as can pure silk or cotton satin provided the latter are subsequently washed only in warm soapy water and not boiled. Stockinet (for sports shirts and shorts) is another possibility worth exploring. Coarse linen, unbleached calico or pure cotton velvet can be used for curtains or other upholstery. Remember though, as a general rule, that the coarser the material the larger the pattern you must use to allow the dye to penetrate properly. Fine material can be gathered quite carelessly and still dye evenly, but similar treatment of a coarse material will tend to disrupt the design.

There are endless variations for tie-dye jackets. In the right-hand model even the border of the pocket adds to the design. The left-hand jacket is complemented by the handbag.

Which dyes to use

As already mentioned, color-fast dyes are best from a practical point of view. These fall into two main categories:

Vat dyes These are the most color- and light-fast and have the widest and richest color range. Unfortunately, they have disadvantages which make them an unwise choice for most people. They are quite complicated to prepare and once prepared require constant attention. They are expensive. The chemicals used with them are potentially dangerous and must be kept well out of reach of young children (this makes them particularly hazardous for teachers to use). Vat dyeing requires a lot of space—more than most people have to spare—and, of course, the choice, as already pointed out, is limited to natural fibers.

Cold-water "reactive" dyes Like vat dyes, these too can only be used with natural fibers. Apart from this, however, they are the ideal choice for tie-dye work. They are not only color- and light-fast and can withstand much hard washing, but they are also simple to use, can be bought in a good range of colors (though not as wide a range as Vat dyes, and for some colors not as rich) and they are relatively inexpensive.

Slightly less color-fast are:

Multipurpose dyes and **liquid instant dyes** Both come in a wide range of colors and, their chief advantage, can be used on most fabrics. They are easy to use and will dye both hot or cold, but only hot dyeing will give a good depth of color.

Instead of dyeing an entire dress begin with a handbag —these patterns are easy to execute. They are lined and have a thin foam-rubber interlining. The bag nearest the camera is a knot batik design.

Top left. A cloak in
unbleached poplin with silk
lining.

Top right. Dressing-gown
in attractive tie-dye design.

Bottom left. The
international, always
modern poncho, easy to sew
and practical.

Long wrap-over skirt, with
head-dress and blouse.

This child's dress in fan
pleating is attractive and
simplicity itself to make.

There are many ways of
positioning the design on
little smocks—this one has a
branching design.

Tie-dyed fabric makes
excellent lampshades, and
the pattern adapts itself to
the shape.

Tie-dye fabric is ideal for
napkins and tray-cloths.
Tea-cosies too are popular
in these days of television.

Hand-made articles for the
home give a personal touch.

A colorful cushion can
brighten up a room without
aspiring to be a work of art.

The basic method

Before you start, a few words of advice. First, always work with *wetted* fabrics. It is always easier to fold material and keep it in position if it is wet. Also, a preliminary washing and rinsing in hot water removes most finishes or glazes and thus facilitates the dyeing process. Second, collect *everything* you need before starting—the reasons for this need not be spelled out! Third, read through the whole of this chapter before embarking on your project to familiarize yourself with the procedure and make sure you understand how the earlier steps affect the later ones and so on. And last but not least—enjoy yourself.

Folding

This, the first stage, determines the general shape or pattern of the design. As already mentioned, if you pleat or fold the material along the line of the weave, or diagonally, for example, you will get stripes or checks. If you fold the material in two then hold it in the center and pleat it up like an umbrella, you will get circular patterns. (It is easier to get an idea of the pattern if, when the material has been folded, the back and front sides are marked with (washable) red crayon and pencil to show where the colors are going to come.) The variations are endless and you will want to experiment for yourself, but first, here are the eleven most common folds, the ones on which the basic designs on pages 26–85 are based:

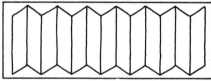

Concertina fold (a) basic type

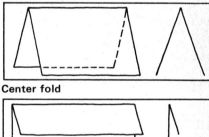

Center fold

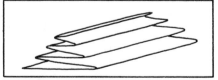

Expanding concertina fold (b) increasing downwards

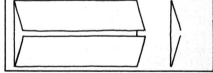

Centrally joined fold

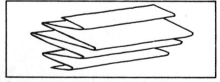

Expanding concertina (c) medial type

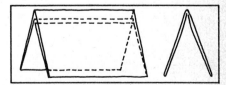

Combined center and centrally joined fold

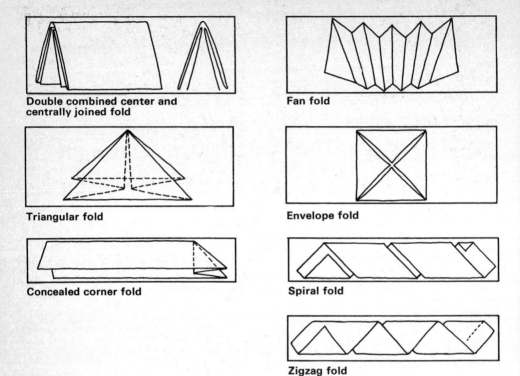

Double combined center and centrally joined fold

Fan fold

Triangular fold

Envelope fold

Concealed corner fold

Spiral fold

Zigzag fold

Fold carefully: any unintended creases may cause uneven distribution of the dye and spoil the general effect of the work however beautiful the colors may be. Do not fold the material so that it becomes bulky and unmanageable: if you do, the dye cannot penetrate the innermost sections.

Equipment for folding and tying.

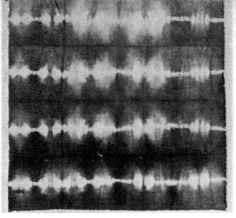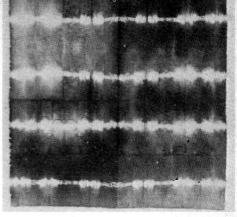

Choosing subjects After the first few experiments this, with the help of the basic design section, will present no problem to you. However, for the complete beginner here are a few suggestions. Start off by making the "center-line" design (I:4, page 28). Then try the "floral border" (I:8, page 30). This could be followed by the "crystal checks" (II:2, page 45) and the "basic circle" (V:I, page 52). This will give you a straightforward but varied start and pave the way for greater things.

Pictures show the importance of folding the material correctly. The cloth on the right is correctly folded. The color is evenly distributed. The material on the left has been folded like a handkerchief and the result is poor.

Tying

This is the "isolating" stage which actually makes the pattern by excluding the dye from parts of the material. The size and nature of the design are determined by where you tie and what you tie with. A coarse thread, for example, gives a thin spidery effect; narrow strips of cloth give broad undyed bands. Always tie tightly unless you are working on a really bulky parcel of material (see page 16). These are some of the most common tying agents:

Coarse thread For thin spidery stripes and net patterns. For net patterns the thread is first wound around in a fairly widely spaced spiral, then to and fro to make an X spiral. The technique is used chiefly for the center of circular designs.

String For stripes of up to 1 inch ordinary white household string should be used; for broader bands a thicker string can be used.

Real and synthetic raffia can be used instead of string (see top illustration on page 17).

Rubber bands are useful for binding gathered tips of material and for securing buttons and other objects (see page 100).

Clothespins Small plastic or wooden pins with a strong clip can be used to produce a dotted pattern. The dots appear wherever the clothespin presses on the folded material (see bottom illustration on page 17).

Rubber blocks, roughly $\frac{1}{2} \times \frac{1}{2}$ inch, can be inserted between the clothespin and the material to give the pattern a softened outline.

Protective cloths The outer layers of the material tend to acquire a rather greater depth of color than the inner ones. To prevent this, take one or more pieces of the material you are using cut to the same measurements as the "parcel" of tied fabric, wrap these around the outside, and secure over the original ties.

Plastic bags are useful for more ambitious projects. The areas to be left undyed are inserted in the bags for protection. Circular strips of plastic can be used as a substitute for really broad string ties. Encase the material to be isolated in the plastic and secure it at each end with a string tie.

Tying thick material The thicker the material and the greater the number of thicknesses involved the greater must be the distance between each "tie" (and the stronger the isolating agent). If you place the "ties" too closely together on thick material the dye will not be able to penetrate properly. When tying bulky parcels of material it is a good idea to place a pencil between the fabric and the isolating agent *before* tying and remove it after tying. This reduces the tension and thus allows the dye to work its way in more easily.

Tying for second and subsequent dyes If a fabric is to be given more than one dye bath it is advisable to isolate not only the undyed areas but also those which are to take the second or subsequent dye only. Similarly, after the first dyeing, isolate the areas which are to take the *first* dye only. If you do not do this, the result will be mixtures rather than clear colors.

Isolating holds

The dyeing instructions given in the basic design section use five different ways of holding the material while dyeing. These are illustrated below. The name in each case is descriptive of the appearance. All five holds are easy to execute.

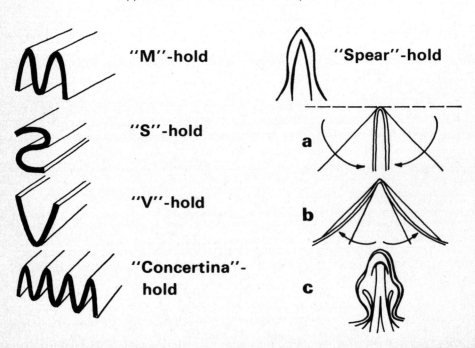

"M"-hold

"Spear"-hold

"S"-hold

a

"V"-hold

b

"Concertina"-
hold

c

By using various types of isolating ties on folded material different patterns of striping can be produced.

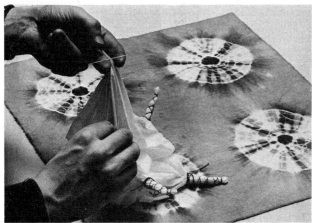

Binding coarse thread ties in an X spiral produces a finely drawn pattern.

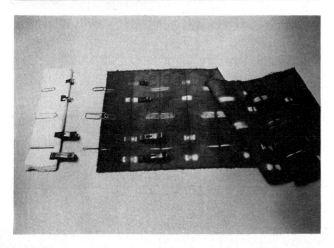

Different types of pegs have been used on this folded material. Clothespins have been used in one instance with little rubber cushions.

Dyeing

This, the final stage, involves dipping the folded tied material into one or more dye baths, depending on the number of colors needed for the design. A certain amount of preparation is required.

Essential equipment Before you start, gather together everything you will need for the project. A large container for the main dye and smaller ones for the contrast dyes (these may be of plastic, china, enamel, stainless steel). A large tub or pail for rinsing. Scissors. Newspapers. A 2 pint measure. A clock. A large apron. Roomy rubber gloves. Soapflakes and saucepan for boiling material after dyeing. An iron. Reliable scales and thermometer if the dye requires precise weighing and temperature (see page 19); a centigrade thermometer is recommended. A pair of large tongs (if you prefer to work without a glove on your right hand). A sieve (for removing undissolved coagulated dye; useful rather than essential). A plastic syringe or oilcan (for squirting the dye into otherwise inaccessible places).

Preparing working surfaces The working area and floor should be covered with newspapers or plastic sheeting for protection (particularly important if you are a beginner). All your equipment should be at hand, and there should be a pile of newspapers for drying off wet material.

Preparing a vat dye Instructions vary in detail from manufacturer to manufacturer and should always be followed implicitly, but the basic procedure is as follows:

A work-table prepared for action.

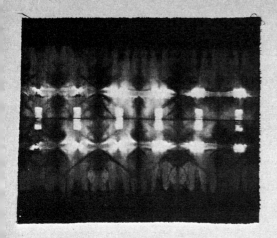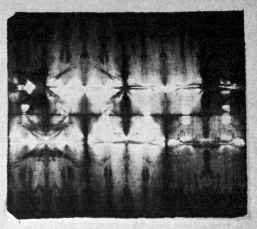

Measure out the correct quantity of dye powder. Mix equal quantities of cold and boiling water to make a temperature of about 55 °C. Stir in the dye, mixing it thoroughly with the water (if the powder does not dissolve completely there is a risk of adhering particles staining the fabric; this can be minimized by mixing the dry powder with a little water to a gruel-like consistency before adding the rest of the water). Stir in approximately half a teaspoon of caustic soda and half a teaspoon of sodium hydrosulphite per pint of water (this will cause the dye to react). Leave until the mixture drops to a temperature of about 30 °C. Once mixed, the solution should be used within the hour, though it is possible to reactivate the dye by replenishing the chemicals.

In tie-dye dyeing the material must be energetically "worked," pinched and twisted. On the left the dyeing has been properly done. On the right the material has not been "worked" at all when immersed in the dye. The material has been folded in half lengthwise and then folded concertina-fashion. A string tie has been placed in the middle and a clothespin clipped on each side of one of the short ends.

Preparing a cold-water dye Again, always follow the manufacturer's instructions implicitly. This is the basic procedure:

Empty the correct amount of powder into a cup or similar vessel and dissolve it with warm water. Dilute in a dye bath filled with the required amount of cold water. Add salt and dissolve this in the solution. Using another cup, dissolve household soda or a cold-water dye fix in a little boiling water and add this to the solution. The dye will now start to react and, as with vat dyes, should be used immediately.

Calculating dye quantities Carefully study the dye manufacturer's directions on the packet. These give instructions as to amounts required. The strength and amount of the contrast dye will depend on the area to be covered. Usually, the water will amount to about a quarter of the foundation bath but relatively more dye may be needed to make a stronger solution. The contrast dye bath needs little liquid—$\frac{1}{2}$ pint should suffice for several dippings. It is no more expensive to use several contrast dyes rather than a large amount of one color—and it is much more exciting! Note To ensure that the foundation dye bath and the contrast dye bath maintain their strength fairly evenly throughout the dyeing process, divide each dye into two batches on starting work and use the second batch of the dye for the second batch of work. Even if a reasonable amount of dye powder seems to be left after the first batch is completed, some of the constituents may in fact have been used up and this could produce a quite different and unlooked-for effect.

The importance of trial pieces The color of a dye varies from material to material, and the printed approximation of a color is often unreliable. It is, therefore, very difficult to visualize how the colors will appear on a material before it is finished—by which time it is usually too late to make improvements. Because of this, it is always advisable to test the color of the dye, the length of dyeing time required and how the colors are going to look in juxtaposition. This can be done by testing on odd pieces of the actual material you are going to use. If the material is to be given *two* dye baths, trial pieces will be needed to show how the colors will appear, first on the areas receiving both dyes, and secondly on those which are isolated after the first dyeing. The more dyes you use the more important it is to test the various reactions at each stage.

Because damp colors are misleading it is best to dry the trial pieces before inspecting the result. Rinse them first under the faucet, squeeze them out in newspapers and then iron them or place near a hot stove. If time is too short for this, a rough idea of the finished result can be got by holding the wet piece up against a window or lamp. It is useful to keep a scrapbook of all successful tie-dyed fabrics with a note on dyes, quantities and dyeing times.

The dyeing process Once the material has been washed, folded and tied, and the dyes have been prepared and tested, dyeing can begin. First wet the material thoroughly (this helps the dye to "take"), then immerse it in the dye bath—for a few minutes if using a vat dye, at least 30 minutes if using a cold-water dye. Squeeze the material horizontally and vertically, turn it carefully both clockwise and anti-clockwise. Work the material vigorously in the dye, opening up all the folds so that the dye really penetrates and the material absorbs the maximum amount of color. Then rinse until the water runs clear and, if the work is to be given only one dye bath, wash it in boiling soapy water. (Ordinary detergents may be used, but avoid enzyme products, which tend to strip the color.) Hang up the work, still tied, to dry. Finally, remove the ties and iron it flat.

Using the contrast dye Once the first or "foundation" dye has been applied certain circumscribed parts of the material may be dipped in one or more strong solutions in a contrasting color. The areas dipped in more than one dye take on different color tones. Even if the first dye is pale in color and does not noticeably affect the color of the second dye a two-tone effect is nevertheless produced. More complicated dyeing requires planning in advance to ascertain which areas are to be dyed and in which

Opposite
(1) Dye in foundation dye.

(2) Rinse well.

(3) Squeeze out water in newspaper.

(4) Remove string tie. Dip the end without clothespins in contrast dye to the point at which the white band left by the string is ½ inch under the surface. Rinse well.

(5) Remove clothespins. Dip the other end in the second contrast dye just far enough to cover the white clothespin marks. Rinse well.

(6) Iron until dry. If retouching is required do so immediately while the dye is still reacting.

1

4

2

5

3

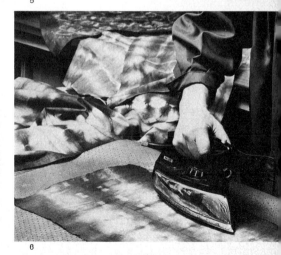

6

colors and where and when the "ties" are to be added or removed as the case may be. Hold the material in one hand while dyeing it and take care not to move the fingers at all as it is only too easy to get unwanted finger-marks. At the same time the tongs should be manipulated so that the color really floods in. For bright "rays" of color hold up the material turning it several times then squeeze out some of the dye or the rays may be over bright.

Usually the fabric is dipped in the dye to within $\frac{1}{2}$ inch of the "tie" which marks the limit of the color. This will result in a decorative border of a darker two-tone shade. Make sure the dye penetrates as completely as possible and that the outer edges of the material are given a little extra dyeing time. For an attractive veined appearance allow the solution at water-level to soak up into the material.

Rinse immediately after each dip. This is essential to ensure that the dyes do not become mixed and the dye itself does not smear. Then squeeze out the wet material in newspapers.

To make a two-tone color band dip the material twice in the contrast dye but only remove the tie after the first dip. The twice-tinted color will then be more intense but the tied area (which will have had one dyeing only—from the second dye) will not be too dark in color.

Injecting the dye If the layers of material to be dipped in the contrast dye are difficult to reach then the dye can be injected into it by means of a syringe or a plastic oilcan. In the last resort it can even be poured in with the aid of a large spoon!

Tinting If part of the material is held in the dye solution longer than the rest a darker shade is obtained. Such tinting gives a greater depth and clarity to the design.

Tie-dyeing is usually more successful if either one or both of the outer edges of the work are given a little extra time in the dye bath. An attractive color effect can also be obtained by dipping each end in a different color for a slightly longer period than the rest of the dyeing.

Retouching On unfolding a piece of fabric you may find that part of it is too pale. If so, refold and tie the material as before and dye the offending part again. This is the only safe method of retouching to ensure that the additional dyeing is similar in character to the rest.

If only very small patches are in question then you may very carefully apply a little color, preferably with a small piece of foam rubber dipped in the dye solution. The material must, however, be wetted first and placed on newspaper.

Toning down colors If there is little blending of colors the effect may be rather too garish. This can be toned down by ensuring that some of the colors cover smaller and some larger areas, or by making some of the colors paler in tone and some darker.

Color considerations

Even if the folding and tying are carried out in exactly the same way the tie-dyed fabric will vary tremendously if the dyes or dipping procedures are altered. The use of strongly contrasting colors in tie-dyeing gives a bold and arresting effect while pastel shades are discreet and subdued. A fabric may be given a strong foundation color with limited detail in another color or several colors may cover larger areas of the fabric. If two contrasting color dye baths are used (for example, violet and orange or turquoise and violet) a further hybrid color is obtained, differing completely from the other two and serving to throw the design into sharp relief. If two closely relating colors are used (for example, yellow and red or green and yellow) the hybrid of these two colors melts into the background and the design itself stands out less clearly. Even if you are not using many different dyes, variety and a more expressive use of color may be obtained by using different shades of the same color. This is done by varying the dyeing times.

Suggestions for two- and three-dye combinations

The following suggestions have been worked out to help the beginner. Tastes naturally vary but these combinations have been found generally pleasing. We have made the first dye bath the lightest in color throughout: using the strongest dye last usually gives the most satisfactory results. If a fabric is to be dyed in light colors only then the palest tone tends to look rather faded. For a light over-all effect the fabric should be broken up with some darker, finely etched lines. For softer, more subdued colors these directions can still be followed but a little dark color should be added to either one or more of the dye baths.

The suggested schemes are subdivided into five groups according to the color of the first dye bath (this usually turns out to be the dominant color in the tie-dyed fabric also).

Group 1
Color accent of the first dye bath is purple/red

	Dye 1	Dye 2	Dye 3
a	amethyst	turquoise	
b	vermilion	turquoise	brown

Group 2
Color accent of the first dye bath is saffron/yellow

	Dye 1	Dye 2	Dye 3
a	yellow	amethyst	dark green or mauve
b	lemon yellow	turquoise	violet or possibly purple

| c | orange yellow or vermilion | mauve | possibly emerald or turquoise |
| d | lemon yellow | vermilion | mauve |

Group 3

Color accent of the first dye bath is brown yellow/brown red

	Dye 1	*Dye 2*	*Dye 3*
a	coffee brown	lemon yellow	amethyst
b	chestnut or coffee brown	turquoise, blue or mauve	

Group 4

Color accent of the first dye bath is green/turquoise

	Dye 1	*Dye 2*	*Dye 3*
a	turquoise	coffee brown	
b	turquoise	orange yellow	violet
c	turquoise	mauve	

Group 5

Color accent of the first dye bath is blue/mauve

	Dye 1	*Dye 2*	*Dye 3*
a	iris or mauve	coffee brown	
b	violet	yellow	dark brown
c	mauve	purple	coffee brown

The color chart as an aid to color choice The circular chart shown is based on three primary colors—red, yellow and blue. In tie-dyeing if two related colors are chosen then, by consulting the chart, it should be easy to predict which color blends the finished fabric will acquire. Colors lying within the same third of the circle are considered to be related—for example, yellow and orange, or yellow and green, or yellow and blue. It must, however, be borne in mind that if one of the two colors is stronger than the other this is the one that will predominate in the resulting color blend. If, for instance, the first dye bath is a fairly light red, and the second dye bath is a medium blue then the resulting blend will be violet. If each of the colors had been of equal strength the result would have been a more neutral mauve. If the colors chosen do not lie within the same third of the circle the resulting blend will have a brownish tinge and in this case it is altogether more difficult to predict the final color blend.

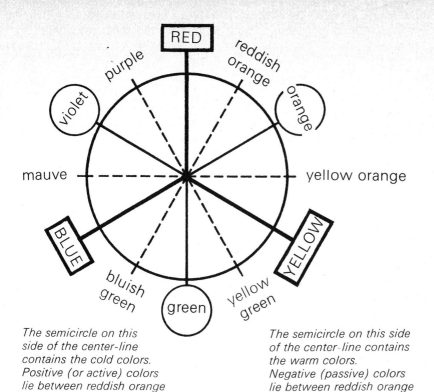

The semicircle on this side of the center-line contains the cold colors. Positive (or active) colors lie between reddish orange and bluish green

The semicircle on this side of the center-line contains the warm colors. Negative (passive) colors lie between reddish orange and bluish green.

Primary colors: red, yellow, blue
Secondary colors: orange, green, violet
Color blends are colors containing at least two of the primary colors. As each of the three sectors which lie between the circle's three primary colors is divided into four, nine color blends in all are obtainable from this.
Complementary colors are those which harmonize with one another.

How to determine complementary colors
(applicable to any part of the circle)

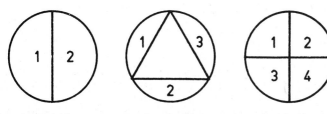

two colors   three colors   four colors

six colors

Basic designs

This section gives detailed instructions for thirteen designs and variations on the basic themes. From them you will be able to develop a rich variety of individual designs and color schemes. The instructions given are based on fairly small measurements, but these can readily be adapted to larger models. The designs have been limited in the first instance to two colors to make the procedure easier to follow, but once you have mastered the technique you may wish to experiment with more ambitious schemes (the section on three-color dye designs will help you with this).

I Stripes

Because the technique of tie-dyeing is particularly suited to striping this type of design is perhaps the commonest. From the examples illustrated in this book it is easy to see that it has immense possibilities. Vertical stripes impose certain limitations: the length of the material can only be so long, because too many thicknesses mean the dye cannot penetrate (except where clothes-pins hold the material in position). Horizontal striping can be as long as you wish. In this case the material is folded lengthwise and the isolating ties are put on horizontally. This is of consequence when it comes to making narrow-width curtaining or tie-dyed fabric by the yard.

I:1 Radar waves

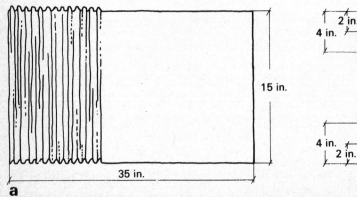

15 in.

35 in.

a

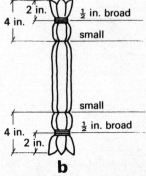

2 in.

4 in.

½ in. broad

small

small

½ in. broad

4 in.

2 in.

b

Size of material 15×35 inches

FOLDING AND TYING

(*a*) Gather the material. (*b*) Bind with isolating string.

DYEING

When the fabric has been dyed in the foundation bath then dip the ends only in the contrast dye to a depth of about 4½ inches. Rinse the work and remove the 2 inch ties. Dip the ends in the contrast dye again to a depth of about 3 inches. See illustration on page 33.

I:2 Rocket glow

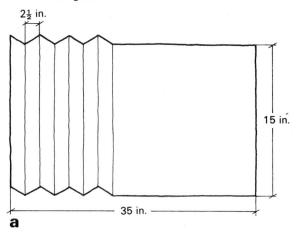

a

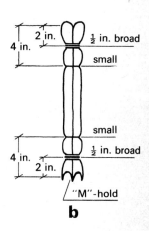

b

Size of material 15×35 inches

FOLDING AND TYING

(*a*) Arrange the material in concertina folds, 2½ inches to each half-pleat. (*b*) Bind with isolating string.

DYEING

After dyeing the fabric in a foundation bath, dip the two ends only in a contrast dye to a depth of about 4½ inches. Rinse the work and remove the 2 inch ties. Dip the ends once more in the contrast dye to a depth of about 3 inches. See illustration on page 33.

I:3 Water reflections

Size of material 15×35 inches

FOLDING AND TYING

(*a*) Fold the material as in I:2. (*b*) Clip eight clothespins over the pleats as shown in diagram. (*c*) After applying the foundation dye clip four clothespins on to the material at the points marked X.

DYEING

After the foundation dye has been applied and the four clothespins clipped on at the points marked X, dip both ends of the material to a depth of about 5½ inches in the contrast dye. Rinse the fabric and remove the clothespins. Dip the ends again in the contrast dye to a depth of about 3½ inches. See illustration on page 33.

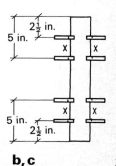

b, c

I:4 Center line pattern

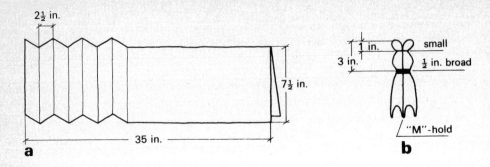

a

b

Size of material 15×35 inches
FOLDING AND TYING
(a) After center-folding the material, pleat it concertina-fashion with seven pleats, each half-pleat measuring $2\frac{1}{2}$ inches. (b) Tie with isolating string.
DYEING
After the foundation dyeing, dip the end with the center fold to a depth of $3\frac{1}{2}$ inches in the contrast dye. Rinse the fabric and remove the 3 inch string tie. Dip the end again in the contrast dye to a depth of $3\frac{1}{2}$ inches. Finally, dip the other end in the contrast dye to a depth of about $1\frac{1}{2}$ inches. See illustration on page 33.

I:5 Ladder pattern

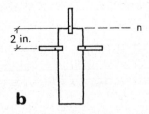

b

Size of material 15×35 inches
FOLDING AND TYING
(a) Fold the material as in I:4. (b) Clip the folds with six clothes-pins.
DYEING
After applying the foundation dye dip the end with the center fold in the contrast dye to a depth of about $2\frac{1}{2}$ inches. Rinse the work and remove the four 2 inch clothespins. Dip the end again in the contrast dye to a depth of about $2\frac{1}{2}$ inches. See illustration on page 34.

I:6 Side lines

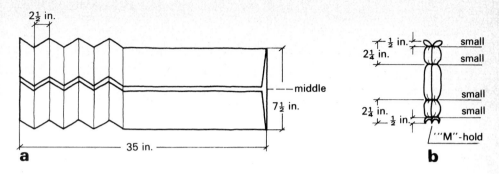

a
2½ in.
middle
7½ in.
35 in.

b
½ in. — small
2¼ in. — small
small
2¼ in. — small
½ in.
'''M''-hold

Size of material 15 × 35 inches

FOLDING AND TYING

(*a*) Centrally-join the material and pleat it concertina-fashion into seven pleats, each half-pleat measuring 2½ inches. (*b*) Tie with isolating string as shown.

DYEING

After the foundation dyeing, dip the ends to a depth of about 2¾ inches in the contrast dye. Rinse the work and remove the 2¼ inch ties. Dip the ends in the contrast dye once more to a depth of about 2¾ inches. See illustration on page 34.

I:7 Flower stripes

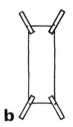

b

Size of material 15 × 35 inches

FOLDING AND TYING .

(*a*) Fold the material as in I:6. (*b*) Clip the folds with eight clothespins.

DYEING

After the foundation dyeing, dip the ends to a depth of about 1¼ inches. See illustration on page 34.

The next three items are all given in sizes suitable for cushion-covers, handbags, table-mats and so on. They have been included as good examples of table-linen patterns. All are decorative and easy to execute—the latter an important consideration if you are intending to make several items in the same pattern.

I:8 Floral border (A)

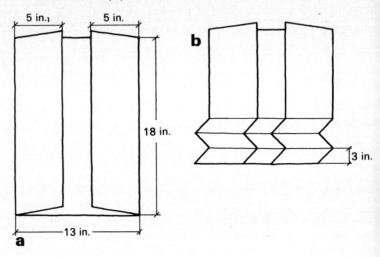

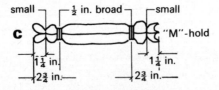

Size of material 18×23 inches

FOLDING AND TYING

(a) Fold the material in a centrally joined fold. (b) Fold again in a concertina fold with three pleats, each half-pleat measuring 3 inches. (c) Tie with isolating string. (d) After foundation dyeing, clip on four clothespins as shown in diagram.

DYEING

Once the four clothespins have been clipped on after the foundation dyeing, dip the ends briefly in the contrast dye to a depth of about $3\frac{1}{4}$ inches. Rinse the work and remove the ties. Finally, dip the ends once more in the contrast dye to about the same depth but leaving 1 inch of the outer edges in the dye a little longer than the rest to acquire a darker shade. See illustration on page 34.

I:9 Floral border (B)

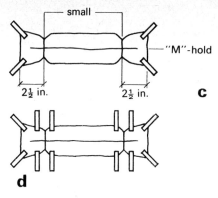

Size of material 18×23 inches

FOLDING AND TYING

(*a*) and (*b*) Fold the material as in I:8. (*c*) Tie with isolating string and clip on four clothespins, one on each corner. (*d*) After foundation dyeing clip on eight more clothespins, one on each side of the ties.

DYEING

Once the eight clothespins have been clipped on after the foundation dyeing, dip the ends in the contrast dye to a depth of about $3\frac{1}{2}$ inches. Rinse the work and remove the ties, together with the first four clothespins. Dip the ends once more in the contrast dye leaving about $\frac{1}{2}$ inch of the outermost edge in the dye twice as long as the rest. See illustration on page 34.

I:10 Floral border (C)

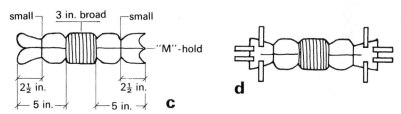

Size of material 18×23 inches

FOLDING AND TYING

(*a*) and (*b*) Fold the material as in I:8. (*c*) Tie with isolating string and a strip of cloth. (*d*) Clip eight clothespins on the ends after the foundation dyeing.

DYEING

Once the eight clothespins have been clipped on after the foundation dyeing, dip the ends in the contrast dye to a depth of about 3 inches. Rinse. Remove the strip of cloth. Hold the sides of the center piece in a spear hold (see page 16) and dip them in the contrast dye to a depth of about $1\frac{3}{4}$ inches. See illustration on page 34.

II Checks

Checks work particularly well if carried out on a scale large enough to show every detail of the design. This is equally true of designs using one color and one tie as of designs using several ties, clothespins and ingenious folds. To achieve a well-wrought check pattern it is advisable not to work with more thicknesses of material than those suggested (too many will make the parcel too bulky). On the other hand the actual *pattern* of the design may be enlarged to allow more scope for variations and original use of color.

II:1 Flowered checks

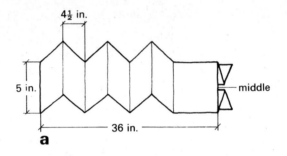

a

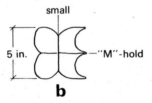

b

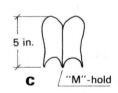

c

Size of material 15×36 inches

FOLDING AND TYING

(*a*) Make a double combined center and centrally joined fold, then fold material concertina-fashion into four pleats, each half-pleat measuring 4½ inches. (*b*) Bind with isolating string, parallel with the concertina edges.

DYEING

After foundation dyeing rinse the material and remove the ties. Hold the material in an M hold (see page 16) the opposite way around, dipping both ends in the contrast dye to a depth of about 1 inch. See illustration on page 35.

I Stripes

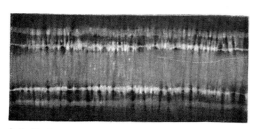

I:1 Radar waves
see page 27

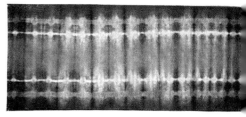

I:2 Rocket glow
see page 27

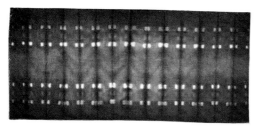

I:3 Water reflections
see page 27

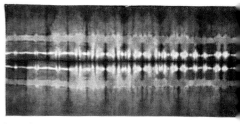

I:4 Center-line pattern
see page 28

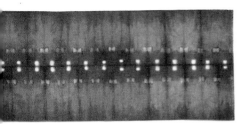

I:5 Ladder pattern
see page 28

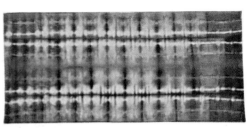

I:6 Side lines
see page 29

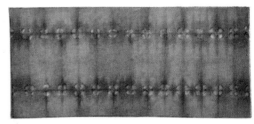

I:7 Flower stripes
see page 29

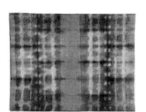

I:8 Floral border (A)
see page 30

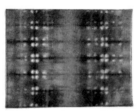

I:9 Floral border (B)
see page 31

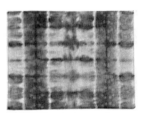

I:10 Floral border (C)
see page 31

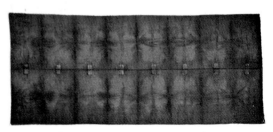

I:11 Creeper pattern
see page 87

II Checks

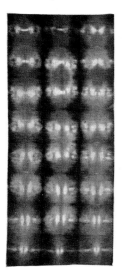

II:1 Flowered checks
see page 32

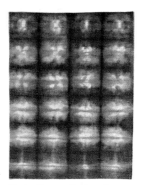

II:2 Crystal checks
see page 45

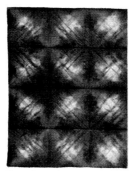

II:7 Star burst pattern
see page 89

II:3 Feathery checks
see page 46

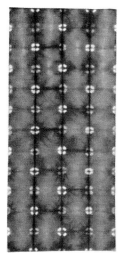

II:4 Corner flower checks
see page 46

II:5 Butterfly checks
see page 47

II:6 Checked garland
see page 47

III Squares

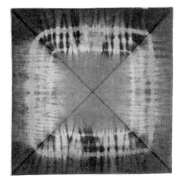

III:1 Basic square
see page 48

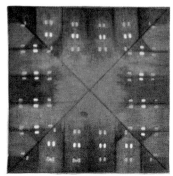

III:2 Four-cornered tower
see page 49

III:3 Flower square
see page 89

IV Rectangles

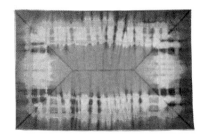

IV:1 Basic rectangle
see page 50

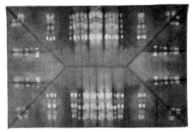

IV:2 Rectangular tower
see page 51

V Circles

V:1 Basic circle
see page 52

V:2 Three-circle pattern
see page 53

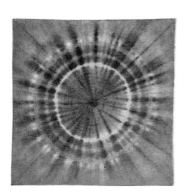

V:3 Sun pattern
see page 54

V:4 Sunbeam pattern
see page 55

VI Ovals

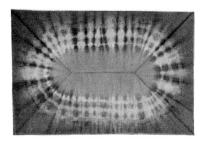 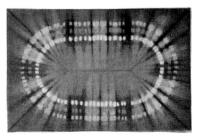

VI:1 Basic oval
see page 56

VI:2 Stadium design
see page 58

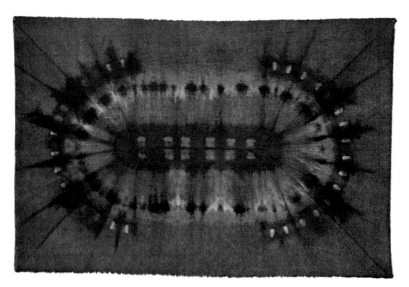

VI:3 Oval flower design
see page 91

VII Diagonal designs

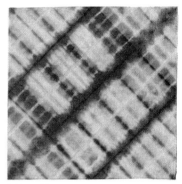

VII:1 Basic diagonal design
see page 59

VII:2 Diagonal flower pattern
see page 60

VII:3 Diagonal square pattern
see page 60

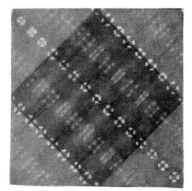

VII:4 Square flower pattern
se page 61

VIII Herringbone designs

VIII:1 Feather pattern
see page 62

VIII:2 VX design
see page 62

VIII:3 Zigzag leaves
see page 62

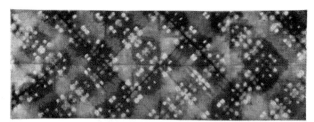

VIII:4 Flower pattern
see page 63

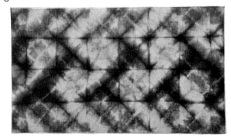

VIII:5 Double herringbone pattern
see page 63

IX Fan-shape designs

IX:1 Basic fan pattern
see page 65

IX:2 Dotted ray pattern
see page 65

IX:3 Peacock pattern
see page 66

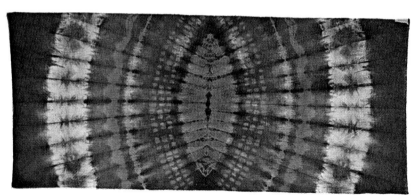

IX:4 Eye pattern
see page 94

X Branching designs

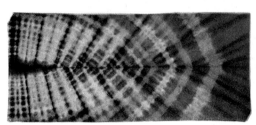

X:1 Branching network pattern
see page 68

X:2 Triangular branching pattern
see page 69

X:3 Branching flower pattern
see page 69

X:4 Pearl necklet pattern
see page 70

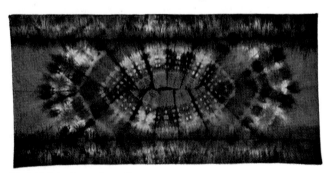

X:6 Triple branch pattern
see page 96

XI Four-cornered designs

XI:1 Four-leaf clover
pattern
see page 73

XI:2 Four-cornered
lattice pattern
see page 75

XI:3 Four-cornered
leaf pattern
see page 76

XI:4 Four-cornered
pattern
see page 77

XI:5 Four-cornered flower pattern
see page 97

XI:6 Four-cornered wreath pattern
see page 97

XII Cross designs

XII:3 Peasant flower
pattern
see page 82

XII:4 Flowering creeper
pattern
see page 98

XII:1 Circular cross XII:2 Flower cross
pattern   pattern
see page 80   see page 80

XIII S-shape designs

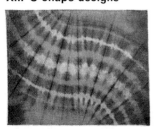

XIII:1 River pattern
see page 84

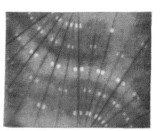

XIII:2 Star pattern
see page 84

XIII:3 Double S pattern
see page 85

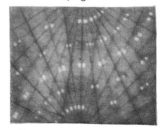

XIII:4 Javanese curves
see page 85

II:2 Crystal checks

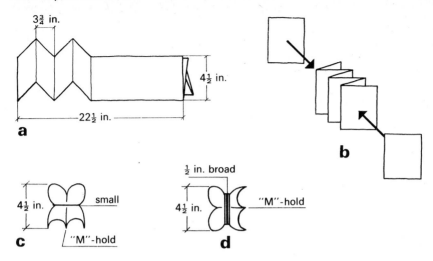

a

b

c "M"-hold

d "M"-hold

½ in. broad

small

4½ in.

3¾ in.

22½ in.

4½ in.

Size of material $17\frac{1}{2} \times 22\frac{1}{2}$ inches

FOLDING AND TYING

(a) Make a center and centrally joined fold, then fold the material concertina-fashion into three pleats, each half-pleat measuring $3\frac{3}{4}$ inches. (b) Put a protective piece of material measuring $3\frac{3}{4} \times 4\frac{1}{2}$ inches on each side. (c) Bind with isolating string (note: insert a pencil before binding as suggested on page 16). (d) Remove tie after foundation dyeing and bind it on again the opposite way around.

DYEING

After the foundation dye dip the whole fabric in the contrast dye. Rinse and remove tie. Bind tie on again the opposite way around and dip fabric in the contrast dye. See illustration on page 35.

II:3 Feathery checks

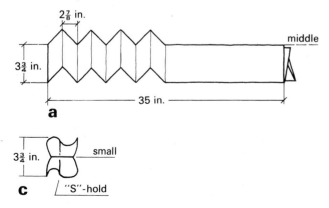

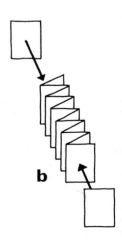

a

b

c "S"-hold

middle

small

$2\frac{7}{8}$ in.

$3\frac{3}{4}$ in.

35 in.

$3\frac{3}{4}$ in.

Size of material 15×35 inches

FOLDING AND TYING

(a) Make a combined center and centrally joined fold, then a concertina fold of six pleats, each half-pleat measuring $2\frac{7}{8}$ inches. (b) Put a piece of protective material measuring $3 \times 3\frac{3}{4}$ inches on each side. (c) Bind with isolating string (note: insert a pencil as suggested on page 16).

DYEING

After the foundation dyeing remove the string. Dip the $3\frac{3}{4}$ inch concertina-folded side in the contrast dye to a depth of about $\frac{1}{2}$ inch. While doing this hold the material at the opposite end in an M hold. Rinse. Fold material concertina-fashion the opposite way around. Finally, dip the same side again in the contrast dye as before. See illustration on page 35.

II:4 Corner flower checks

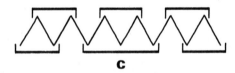

c

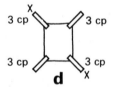

d

e

Size of material 15×35 inches

FOLDING AND TYING

(a) and (b) Fold the material and place on the protective cloths as in II:3. (c) Clip the pleats together with twelve clothespins at the corners. The diagram shows how the pleats are distributed when the clothespins are placed in position. (d) Front view of material. (e) Hold the material piece together with loosely tied string.

DYEING

After the foundation dyeing, dip the four corners in the contrast dye to a depth of about 1 inch. Rinse. Remove the six clothespins at the points marked X. Finally, dip the four corners once more in the contrast dye to a depth of about 1 inch. See illustration on page 35.

II:5 Butterfly checks

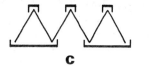

c

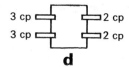

d

Size of material $17\frac{1}{2} \times 22\frac{1}{2}$ inches

FOLDING AND TYING

(*a*) and (*b*) Fold the material and place on the protective cloths as in II:2. (*c*) Clip the pleats together with 10 clothespins. The diagram shows how the pleats are distributed when the clothespins are placed in position. (*d*) Front view of material.

DYEING

After applying the foundation dye dip the concertina-folded sides measuring $3\frac{3}{4}$ inches in the contrast dye to a depth of about 1 inch, holding the material in the middle with an M hold. Rinse. Remove the clothespins and dip the material once again in the contrast dye in the same way as before. See illustration on page 35.

II:6 Checked garland

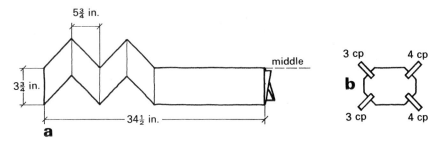

Size of material $15 \times 34\frac{1}{2}$ inches

FOLDING AND TYING

(*a*) Make a combined center and centrally joined fold, then make a concertina fold of three pleats, each half-pleat measuring $5\frac{3}{4}$ inches. (*b*) Make each corner into a concealed corner, fold and clip on a clothespin (fourteen clothespins in all).

DYEING

After the foundation dyeing, dip each of the four corners in the contrast dye to a depth of about 1 inch. Rinse the work, remove the clothespins and corner folds. Finally, dip the short $3\frac{3}{4}$ inch ends in the contrast dye to a depth of about 1 inch, holding the work in an M hold. See illustration on page 35.

For a more even striping than shown in the illustration, refold the material concertina-fashion in the opposite direction and dip the short ends once more to a depth of about 1 inch in the contrast dye.

47

III Squares

Unlike check patterns squares are built up from only one square. To make a square pattern the material itself must be square, which is not as useful a shape as oblong. A long, narrow model needs a rectangular pattern which may be more or less as long as you like (see page 50). Both rectangular and square designs can include ingenious corner folds. Corner folding may be used on most designs with horizontal striping. In such cases the stripes do not appear to be cut off abruptly but, on the contrary, well finished. Corner folding is particularly useful when making clothes. For instance, to make a pattern for a dress that opens all the way down, cut the material in two after dyeing and use the two outside borders as the overlapping edges of the center opening. A square design combines well with a rectangular one, for example, as a pocket on a striped dress. It is also effective in smaller sizes for such items as cloths and table-napkins.

III:1 Basic square

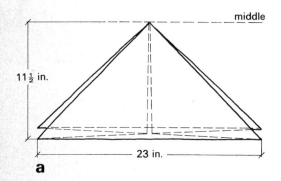

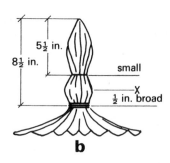

Size of material 23×23 inches

FOLDING AND TYING

(a) Make first a center fold then a triangular fold. (b) Gather the material and bind with isolating string.

DYEING

After the foundation dyeing bind around a third string at X. Hold the material by the tip and dip it in the contrast dye so that only 5 inches protrude above the surface. Rinse the work and remove the first two string ties (but not the one at X). Dip the material in the contrast dye again in the same way, giving the outer edges a rather stronger color. See illustration on page 36.

III:2 Four-cornered tower

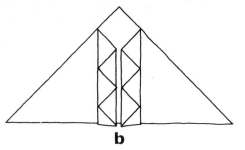

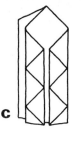

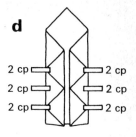

d

c

b

2 cp ▭⎯ ⎯▭ 2 cp
2 cp ▭⎯ ⎯▭ 2 cp
2 cp ▭⎯ ⎯▭ 2 cp

Size of material 23×23 inches

FOLDING AND TYING

(*a*) Fold as in III:1. (*b*) Fold concertina-fashion first the one then the other layer of material, as shown in the diagram on page 13. (*c*) Turn the work around and fold the other side similarly. (*d*) Clip three clothespins on each side, back and front (twelve clothespins in all).

DYEING

After the foundation dyeing, hold the material by the tip and dip it in the contrast dye as far as the topmost clothespins. Rinse. Remove all except the four middle clothespins. Dip the material again in the contrast dye as far as the marks left by the topmost clothespins. Dip again in the contrast dye to give the outer edges a darker color. See illustration on page 36.

III:3 Flower square

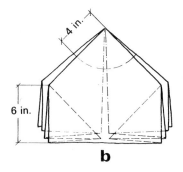

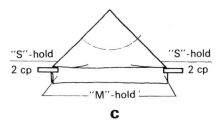

4 in.

6 in.

"S"-hold   "S"-hold

2 cp ▭⎯   ⎯▭ 2 cp

"M"-hold

b   **c**   **d**

Size of material 23×23 inches

FOLDING AND TYING

(*a*) Fold as in III:1. (*b*) Fold the four bottom corners into concealed corners and draw a part-circle in washable crayon as shown in diagram. (*c*) Hold the 6 inch corners in an M hold and clip a clothespin on to each to hold it in position (four clothespins in all). Flatten and arrange the material as shown in diagram and then make an S hold as far down as possible on each of the two slanting sides. Clip in position with clothespins. Altogether there will be six clothespins. (*d*) Gather together the top along the

49

marked part-circle and bind around isolating string to a width of $\frac{1}{2}$ inch. Finally make an X spiral of coarse thread from the top and downward for $1\frac{1}{2}$ inches.

DYEING

After foundation dyeing, dip the top in contrast dye until the string is just below the surface. After rinsing remove the thread and the string. Dip the same part once again to the same depth in the contrast dye. Straighten the folds held by the clothespins and then dip each side separately in the contrast dye, holding the material gathered up just below the clothespin and dipping it until the dye just covers the clothespins. Rinse the work and remove the clothespins. Then, holding the material in the same way again dip this same piece of the material once more in the contrast dye. See illustration on page 36.

IV Rectangles

IV:1 Basic rectangle

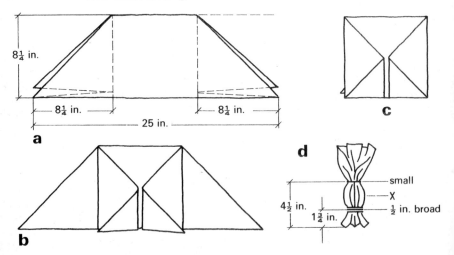

Size of material $16\frac{1}{2} \times 25$ inches

FOLDING AND TYING

(a) Make first a center fold then a concealed corner fold. (b) Concertina-fold first the right-hand side then the left-hand side of the top layer as shown in diagram. (c) Turn the work over and fold the other side in the same way. (d) Gather the material and bind it with isolating string (note: insert a pencil as described on page 16 before binding).

DYEING

After the foundation dyeing make a third tie at X. Hold the work by the center fold and dip it in the contrast dye so that only 3 inches protrude above the surface. Rinse. Remove both the outer ties (but not the tie at X). Dip the work once more in the contrast dye in the same way, making the outer edges a little darker. See illustration on page 36.

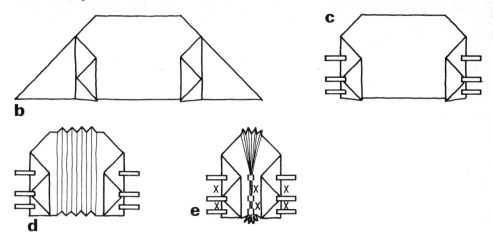

Size of material $16\frac{1}{2} \times 25$ inches

FOLDING AND TYING

(*a*) Fold as in IV:1. (*b*) Fold first the one then the other side of the top layer of cloth concertina-fashion as shown in the diagram. (*c*) Turn the work over and fold the other side in the same way. Clip three clothespins on to each side, both front and back (twelve clothespins in all). (*d*) Make four pleats in the center. (*e*) Hold the folds in position, both front and back, and at the same level as the others (altogether there are now eighteen clothespins).

DYEING

After the foundation dyeing place a further twelve clothespins between the others at the points marked X. Altogether there are now thirty clothespins. Hold the material by the center fold and dip it in the contrast dye up to the level of the top row of clothespins. Rinse. Remove the first eighteen clothespins, leaving only the twelve clothespins which were placed last at the points marked X. Dip the work in the contrast dye to the level of the marks of the top clothespins, giving the outer edges a rather darker color. See illustration on page 36.

V Circles

Circles are particularly easy. They can be either large or small, they can be placed anywhere and need not take account of one another or of the material's measurements. Circular table-cloths, with just one large encircling design, can look extremely effective. Round chair-covers and cushions look especially good if the design of the material harmonizes with their shape.

V:1 Basic circle

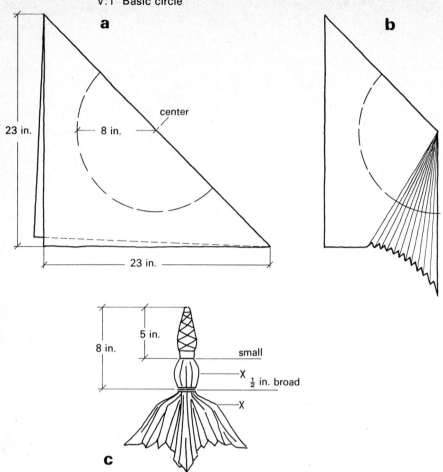

Size of material 23×23 inches

FOLDING AND TYING

(*a*) Fold the material into a triangle and then draw a semi-circle with a radius of 8 inches. (*b*) Hold the material at the center of the circle and pleat. (*c*) Bind with string as shown in the diagram. After foundation dyeing take a coarse thread and bind it in a spiral (not too close together) around the peak of the material, then add two further ties at X.

DYEING

After the foundation dyeing, follow the tying instructions in (*c*). Then dye the whole piece in the contrast dye, giving the tip longer in the dye than the rest of the material. Rinse. Remove the 8 inch tie only. Finally, dip the fabric in the contrast dye once more, tip first, and deep enough for the lowest of the ties to be $\frac{1}{2}$ inch beneath the surface. See illustration on page 37.

V:2 Three-circle pattern

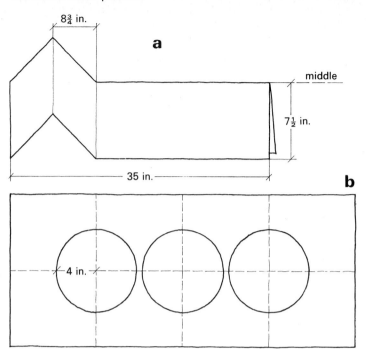

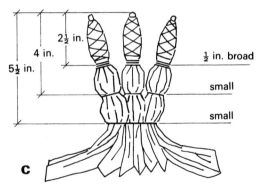

Size of material 15×35 inches

Interlocking circles are attractive, even on large pieces of work such as curtains and large table-cloths. This design is nearly always pleasing because the rays are evenly divided owing to the particular way in which the material has been folded.

FOLDING AND TYING

(*a*) First make a center fold and then pleat concertina-fashion in two pleats, each half-pleat measuring $8\frac{3}{4}$ inches. (*b*) Spread out the material and draw three circles 4 inches in radius with each circle's center at the center of the crosses formed by the folding (see diagram). Remake the center fold. (c) Gather the circles, from the center of each separately, and bind each with string in two places as in diagram. Then bind the three points together as in diagram. After the foundation dyeing bind these three points in an X spiral with coarse thread (not too close together).

DYEING

After the foundation dyeing, bind as instructed in (c). Then dip the material, points downward, in the contrast dye so that the tie that binds all three together comes $\frac{1}{2}$ inch under the surface of the liquid. After rinsing the work remove the three ties. Finally, dip the material points downward again in the contrast dye to the same depth but for longer, so that the tops become darker in color. See illustration on page 37.

The following two designs differ from V:I in that the rays are more evenly distributed. This can have its advantages, especially in large-scale projects, for which you may be less willing to chance the outcome of haphazard pleating. At the same time, because of the folding technique used in these designs, a spear hold (see page 16) may be used which greatly enhances the appearance of the design. For a dotted pattern using clothespins it is *essential* to fold according to the following instructions.

V:3 Sun pattern

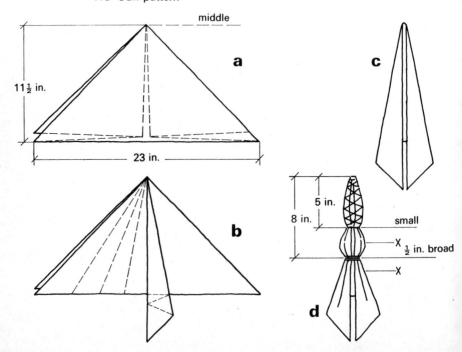

Size of material 23×23 inches
FOLDING AND TYING
(a) Make first a center fold then a triangular fold. (b) Make two pleats out of the top layer right- and left-hand wings of the triangle (note: if these are correctly made the two corners will look like the diagram). (c) Turn the work over and fold the other side in the same way. (d) Tie with string as shown in the diagram. After foundation dyeing bind the point with coarse thread in an X spiral (not too close together). Add two further ties at X.
DYEING
After foundation dyeing, tie as in (d). Then immerse the fabric in the contrast dye, giving the tips a little longer than the rest. Rinse. Remove the 8 inch tie only. Finally, dip the work once more point first in the dye so that the top tie is $\frac{1}{2}$ inch under the surface. See illustration on page 37.

V:4 Sunbeam pattern

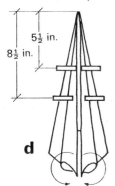
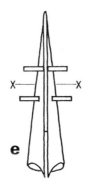

Size of material 23×23 inches
FOLDING AND TYING
(a) to (c) Fold the material as in V:3. (d) Clip together the two top pleats on each side as in diagram (four in all) at the same time turning in the pleats so that their edges point downward. (e) Turn the work over and proceed similarly on remaining sides. Altogether eight clothespins will have been placed in position.
DYEING
After foundation dyeing clip an additional clothespin on each quarter of the material at X (there will now be twelve clothespins altogether). Hold work by the point and dip in the contrast dye to $\frac{1}{2}$ inch above the top clothespins. Rinse. Remove the $5\frac{1}{2}$ inch and $8\frac{1}{2}$ inch clothespins, leaving only the four middle clothespins. Finally, dip the work in the dye to the same depth, giving the outer edges a deeper coloring. See illustration on page 37.

VI Ovals
Oval designs are particularly effective for oval table-cloths, especially large ones. The measurements given here are suitable for small cloths or, if halved, for tea-cosies, bags and pockets on striped clothes.

VI:1 Basic oval (A)

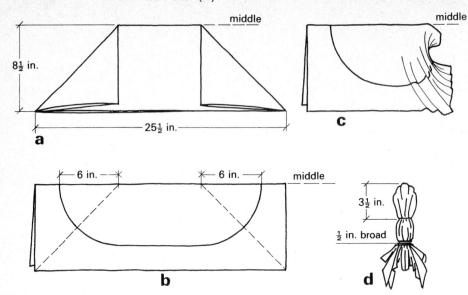

Size of material 17×25 inches

FOLDING AND TYING

(a) Fold the material horizontally then turn in the corners. (b) Unfold the corners and with a pencil draw two quarter-circles each with a 6 inch radius and with the center at X. Draw a straight line joining the two quarter-circles as in diagram. (c) Gather the material along the pencil line. (d) Bind with isolating string where the gathering ends along the pencil line. Bind an additional tie $3\frac{1}{2}$ inches from the center fold.

DYEING

After foundation dyeing, place a third tie between the $3\frac{1}{2}$ inch and the 6 inch ties. Then hold the material by the top and dip in the contrast dye to $\frac{1}{2}$ inch above the $3\frac{1}{2}$ inch tie. Rinse. Remove the $3\frac{1}{2}$ and 6 inch ties leaving the middle one. Finally, dip the material once more to the same depth, giving the outer edges rather longer. See illustration on page 38.

VI:1 Basic oval (B)

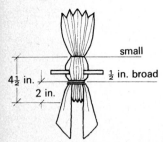

Size of material 17×25 inches

FOLDING AND TYING

For alternative B of the basic oval place clothespins only at the points marked X (four altogether) and bind ties on each of these. Remove the four clothespins before dyeing. Follow dyeing instructions given in VI:IA.

VI:2 Stadium design

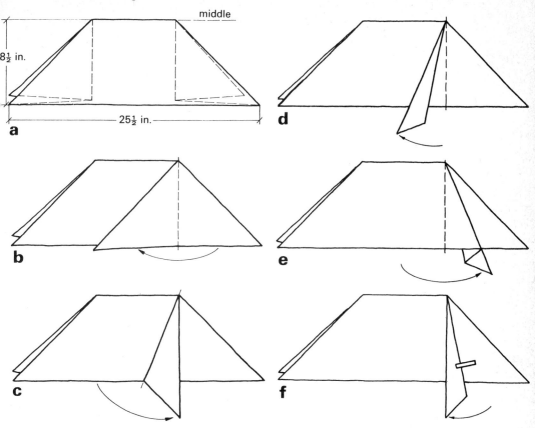

Use this for large projects involving oval designs or for especially even coloring.

Size of material $17 \times 25\frac{1}{2}$ inches.

FOLDING AND TYING

(*a*) Make first a center fold then a concealed corner fold. (*b*) Fold the right side of the top layer as in diagram. (*c*) Fold once more as in diagram. (*d*) Fold the point to the left. (*e*) Turn the "wing" to the right. (*f*) Turn the wing to the left, moving both the outward slanting sides to a position at right angles to the bottom edge. Clip these small pleats together on the outer side. (*g*) Fold the front left-hand side in the same way. (*h*) Turn the work back to front and proceed in the same way on this side. (*i*) Fold the four wings down the center so that the slanting outer edges lie on top of the perpendicular inner edges. Remove the four clothespins (placed on as directed in (*f*), (*g*) and (*h*)). Clip on two more clothespins to hold each of the four wings in position (eight clothespins in all). (*j*) Make three pleats in the middle and hold them in place with two clothespins, on both the front and the

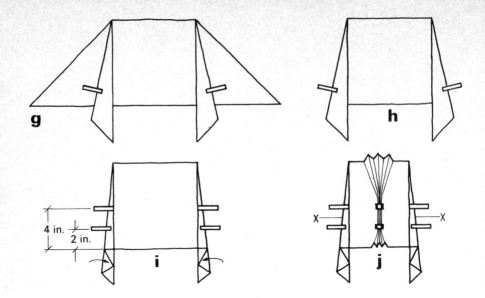

g **h**

4 in. — 2 in.

i **j**

X — — X

back—and place them all in line with the earlier clothespins added as directed in (*i*). Altogether there will be twelve clothespins.

DYEING

After the foundation dyeing, clip on a further six pegs between the 4 inch and 2 inch clothespins (at X). Hold the work by the center fold and dip it in the contrast dye to a depth of $\frac{1}{2}$ inch above the upper clothespins. Rinse. Remove the 4 inch and 2 inch clothespins so that only the six middle clothespins remain. Finally, dip the material once more in the dye to the same depth allowing the outer edges to acquire a darker color. See illustration on page 38.

VI:3 Oval flower design

Size of material $17 \times 25\frac{1}{2}$ inches

FOLDING AND TYING

(*a*) to (*h*) Fold material as in VI:2 (*a*) to (*h*). (*i*) Make three pleats along the center fold and secure them with a clothespin on the center fold. (*j*) Gather the material and bind with a strip of cloth, isolating some 2–$2\frac{1}{2}$ inches.

DYEING

After foundation dyeing, remove the two 5 inch clothespins on the one side, draw up the material into a spear hold at the point at which the white dots appear, then dip it to a depth of about $\frac{1}{2}$ inch in the contrast dye. Treat the other side in the same way. Remove the cloth strip and dip the material peak downward to a depth of about $3\frac{1}{2}$ inches in the contrast dye. Finally, remove the clothespin and dip the point in the contrast dye to a depth of $2\frac{1}{2}$ inches. See illustration on page 38 (note: the fabric in the illustration has been given two dyeings).

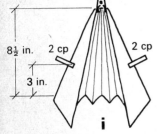

$8\frac{1}{2}$ in. 2 cp   2 cp

3 in.

i

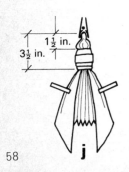

$1\frac{1}{2}$ in.

$3\frac{1}{2}$ in.

j

VII Diagonal designs

Diagonal designs have very specialized characteristics, and are therefore of limited use. They make good trimmings, dresses and scarfs.

VII:1 Basic diagonal design

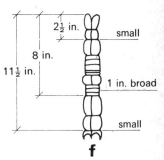

Size of material $17\frac{1}{2} \times 48$ inches

FOLDING AND TYING

(*a*) Find the center of the long side of the material and fold half of it downward. (*b*) Fold the other half upward (using a spiral fold). (*c*) Turn the work over and fold the corners inward. (*d*) Pleat the material concertina-fashion into six pleats, each half-pleat measuring $2\frac{1}{2}$ inches, and place a protective cloth, measuring $2\frac{1}{2} \times 12$ inches, on each side. (*e*) Bind with isolating string and a strip of cloth. (*f*) After foundation dyeing, bind on two more strings and another cloth strip (altogether there will be four string ties and two cloth strips).

DYEING

After the foundation dyeing, bind on ties as described in (*f*). Then dip the whole fabric in the contrast dye. Rinse. Remove the two cloth strips and the $1\frac{1}{2}$ inch and 10 inch ties. Then dip the end which has only the $2\frac{1}{2}$ inch tie remaining in the contrast dye to a depth of 3 inches and the end with the $11\frac{1}{2}$ inch tie to a depth of $2\frac{1}{2}$ inches. Then dip each side of the white band in turn in the contrast dye, holding it in a spear hold. Rinse. Unfold the concertina pleats and refold them the opposite way around. Finally, dip both sides of the 2 inch band in the contrast dye, holding the work in the same spear hold as earlier. See illustration on page 39.

59

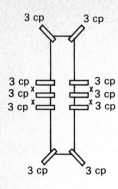

3 cp   3 cp

3 cp   3 cp
3 cp x   x 3 cp
3 cp x   x 3 cp

3 cp   3 cp

VII:2 Diagonal flower pattern

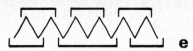

e

Size of material 17½ × 48 inches
FOLDING AND TYING
(a) to (d) Fold the material and protect it with cloths as described in VII:1 (a) to (d). (e) Clip the pleats together with clothespins. The diagram shows how the clothespins are distributed.
DYEING
After the foundation dyeing, place an additional 12 clothespins in the center, three at each point marked X. Then dip this middle section in the contrast dye so that only 3½ inches of the fabric's ends are above the surface of the dye. Rinse. Dip the middle section in the contrast dye again. Finally, dip both the outer edges to a depth of about ¾ inch, giving about ¼ inch of the outer edges a longer time in the dye. See illustration on page 39.

VII:3 Diagonal square pattern

Size of material 23 × 23 inches
The method of folding used in this design is very simple and seldom results in failure regardless of the size of the project. It is particularly suitable for large items because it can be carried out comparatively quickly and is attractive on a large scale.

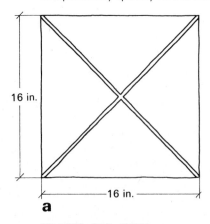

16 in.

16 in.

a

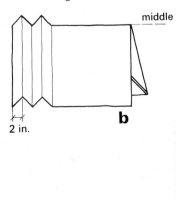

middle

2 in.

b

FOLDING AND TYING
(a) Fold the material envelope-fashion. (b) First make a center fold, then fold concertina-fashion with four pleats, each half-pleat measuring 2 inches. (c) Bind with isolating string.
DYEING
After the foundation dyeing, bind on an additional two ties at X. Then dip the whole in the contrast dye. Rinse. Remove the first three of the ties, leaving only the ties at X. Finally, dip the whole fabric once more in the contrast dye, giving ¼ inch of the ends longer than the rest. See illustration on page 39.

1¼ in.   small

4 in.
              X
              small

              X
              small

1¼ in.

c   "M"-hold

VII:4 Square flower pattern

Size of material 23×23 inches
This design has the same advantages as the preceding one, except that working with clothespins is a little more complicated than working with string. Try combining the two.

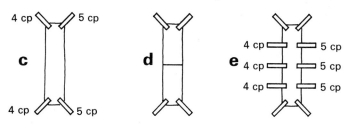

FOLDING AND TYING
(a) and (b) Fold as in VII:3. (c) Fasten the pleats with clothespins at the corners (eighteen in all). (d) Tie a loose noose of string around the middle.

DYEING
After the foundation dyeing, remove the string and clip an additional twenty-seven clothespins on to the middle portion as shown in diagram (e). Dip the fabric in the contrast dye and rinse. Remove the eighteen corner clothespins and dip the fabric once more in the contrast dye. See illustration on page 39.

VIII Herringbone designs

These designs work particularly well on curtains and dresses. They are not as good for trimmings because the pattern gives the impression of having a top and a bottom. This is inevitable as the cloth has to be folded double in the first instance to obtain a mirror image.

VIII:1 Feather pattern

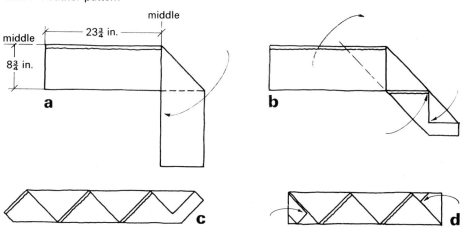

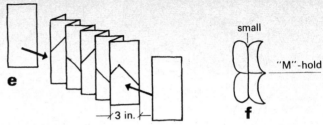

Size of material $17\frac{1}{2} \times 47\frac{1}{2}$ inches

FOLDING AND TYING

(a) Make a center fold and on the front of the material draw a line about 1 inch beneath the fold. Mark the middle of the material and fold one half downward. (b) Make a series of zigzag folds. (c) If the material is properly folded the penciled line will only be visible in the alternate triangles. (d) Fold in the pointed ends. (e) Fold the material concertina-fashion in five pleats, each half-pleat measuring 3 inches, so that each triangle has a pleat in the middle. Put a protective cloth, measuring 3×6 inches, on each side. (f) Bind with isolating string (note: insert a pencil before binding).

DYEING

After the foundation dyeing, remove the tie. Then, using an M hold, dip one of the long sides to a depth of $1-1\frac{1}{2}$ inches in the contrast dye, holding the material at the most furtherly point of the opposite side to ensure that the dye penetrates into the inner-most fold. Give the outermost edges a little extra dyeing time. See illustration on page 40.

VIII:2 VX design

Size of material $17\frac{1}{2} \times 47\frac{1}{2}$ inches

FOLDING AND TYING

(a) to (e) Fold the material and put on protective cloths as in VIII:1. (f) Bind with isolating string (note: insert a pencil before binding). (g) After foundation dyeing, tie as in diagram.

DYEING

After foundation dyeing bind with isolating ties as in diagram (g). Then dip fabric in the contrast dye and rinse. Remove both $1\frac{1}{2}$ inch ties and dip the material once more in the contrast dye, giving the ends a somewhat longer dyeing time. See illustration on page 40.

VIII:3 Zigzag leaves

Size of material $17\frac{1}{2} \times 47\frac{1}{2}$ inches

FOLDING AND TYING

(a) to (f) Fold, put on protective cloths and bind with two isolating ties as in VIII:2. (g) Bind ties around the ends after the foundation dyeing.

DYEING

Having bound ties around the ends as in (g) after foundation dyeing dip first one then the other end in the contrast dye to a depth of 2 inches. Rinse. Remove both the $1\frac{1}{2}$ inch ties. Dip the ends again to a depth of 2 inches in the dye, giving $\frac{1}{2}$ inch of the outer edges a longer dyeing time. See illustration on page 40.

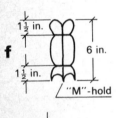

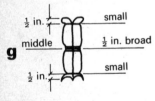

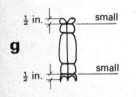

VIII:4 Flower pattern

f

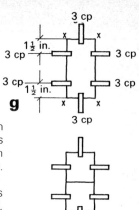

g

Size of material $17\frac{1}{2} \times 47\frac{1}{2}$ inches

FOLDING AND TYING

(a) to (e) Fold the material and place on protective cloths as in VIII:1 (a) to (e). (f) Hold the folds in position with clothespins (eighteen altogether) which should be distributed as shown in diagram. (g) Front view. (h) Tie string loosely around the middle.

DYEING

After foundation dyeing, clip on an additional twelve clothespins at X. Remove the string and, holding the work in an M hold, dip both the short ends in the contrast dye to a depth of $1\frac{3}{4}$ inches. After rinsing the work remove the first eighteen clothespins, leaving only the twelve at X. Holding the work in an M hold dip the ends once more in the contrast dye to a depth of $1\frac{3}{4}$ inches. See illustration on page 40.

h

VIII:5 Double herringbone pattern

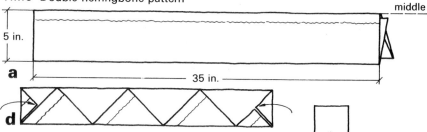

a

d

Size of material 20×35 inches

The double herringbone pattern is best carried out on a largish scale, especially if it is given a three-dye coloring (see section on three-color dye designs). An interesting effect is produced by the irregular diagonal checks and, because the pattern is restrained, it is a particularly good one for curtains.

FOLDING AND TYING

(a) to (c) Make a combined center and centrally joined fold, then draw a line on the front about 1 inch below the fold (see diagram (a). Next, fold zigzag fashion as described in VIII:1 (a) to (c). (d) Turn in the pointed ends. (e) Fold the material concertina-fashion into three and a half pleats, each half-pleat measuring $3\frac{1}{2}$ inches, so that each triangle has a pleat in the middle. Place protective cloths measuring $3\frac{1}{2} \times 3\frac{1}{2}$ inches on each side. (f) Bind with isolating string (note: insert a pencil before tying).

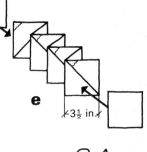

e

f   small

"S"-hold

DYEING

After the foundation dyeing, remove the tie. Then, holding the material firmly in the center with the thumb and middle finger, dip the four sides to a depth of $\frac{1}{4}$ to $\frac{1}{2}$ inch in the contrast dye. See illustration on page 40. Note: as the material is folded into so many layers use only fine materials so that the dye can penetrate.

IX Fan-shape designs

In fan-shape designs the characteristic "raying" should be used to greatest effect for decorative purposes. For this reason it is a good idea to use fan-shape designs for conical-shaped work, such as dresses and skirts. It is also good for handbags, tea-cosies and so on. If the material is first folded the design comes out in a mirror-image form. This gives an "eye" where the material has been folded. The design is excellent both for trimmings and for wall-decorations.

IX:1 Basic fan pattern

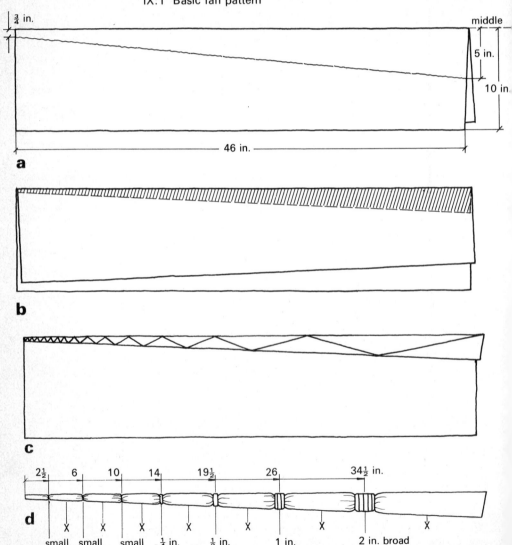

Size of material 20×46 inches

FOLDING AND TYING

(a) Make a center fold and mark out a slanting line to show where the first fold comes. (b) Fold the top layer in such a way that it follows the center-line fold. The shaded area shows the inner fold. (c) Fold the rest of the top layer of material matching the first pleat. Even if the folded material does not look exactly like the diagram this will not affect the final outcome very much. Turn the material over and fold the other side in the same way. (d) Bind with isolating string, except at the 2 inch point where a strip of cloth should be used. The width of the ties should be varied as indicated in the diagram. (e) Fold in an expanding concertina-fashion so that the ties come in the middle. Loosely tie a string around the whole (diagram (e) shows the work as seen from above).

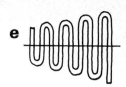

DYEING

After the foundation dyeing, bind with string and strips of cloth at X and, as before, gradually increase the width of the strips. Fold the material again in expanded concertina-fashion and dip the whole in the contrast dye. Rinse. Remove the seven ties which were made first. Finally, dip the fabric once more in the contrast dye giving the section marked off by the broadest tie the longest dyeing period. See illustration on page 41.

IX:2 Dotted ray pattern

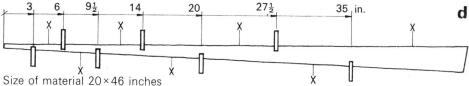

Size of material 20×46 inches

FOLDING AND TYING

(a) to (c) Fold material as in IX:1. (d) Clip the pleats together with clothespins (seven in all). (e) Fold as in IX:1 (e).

DYEING

After the foundation dyeing, place an additional seven clothespins at X. Dip the fabric in the contrast dye and rinse. Remove the seven clothespins placed first. Dye the fabric again, giving the end with the greatest distance between the clothespins the longest dyeing time. See illustration on page 41.

IX:3 Peacock pattern

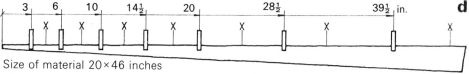

Size of material 20×46 inches

FOLDING AND TYING

(a) to (c) Fold the material as in IX:1. (d) Clip together the pleats with seven clothespins. (e) Pack up material as in IX:1 (e). (f) Material as seen from the front. The clothespins are all on the upper side.

DYEING

After the foundation dyeing, place an additional seven clothes-pins at X. Fold the material once more as in IX:1(e) but this time the side on which the clothespins are placed must be kept flat (see diagram (f)). Then dip the even side (the clothespin side) to a depth of about $\frac{1}{2}$ inch in the contrast dye. Rinse. Remove the initial seven clothespins and repeat the dyeing procedure. Then unfold the concertina folds and examine the edges. Some areas along the pleats will have been insufficiently dyed and will need redoing. Refold just these sections and dip them in the dye once more. See illustration on page 41.

Note: when tie-dyeing large areas it is a good idea to divide up the long side and dye in stages. If the difference in width between the pleats' upper and lower edges is very marked a prettier effect will be achieved if the edges are dipped progressively deeper in the dye as the pleat grows wider.

IX:4 Eye pattern

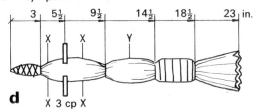

Size of material 20×46 inches

FOLDING AND TYING

(a) to (c) Fold the material in two so that it measures 20×23 inches. Then fold it as in IX:1 (a) to (c), but instead of taking a 5 inch starting-point for the slanting line, substitute a 3 inch one instead. (d) Bind with coarse thread ties and place the clothes-pins, string and cloth strip as shown in diagram.

DYEING

After the foundation dyeing place a $\frac{1}{2}$ inch wide string tie at Y and clip on a further twelve clothespins at X. Altogether there should be eighteen clothespins. Then dip the fabric, peak down-ward, to a depth of 19 inches in the contrast dye. Remove the coarse thread, the first six clothespins to be placed and the $9\frac{1}{2}$ inch tie, then dip the fabric again in the same way in the contrast dye. Remove the cloth strip. Make up the two white edges separately into a spear hold and dip them to a depth of 1 inch in the dye. See illustration on page 41.

X Branching designs

These designs are also suitable for dresses and they make attrac-tive wall-hangings. Secondary patterns may be added to the basic designs (rings, for example) and at least one end may be dyed a deeper shade. Interesting shapes may be obtained by folding the material in two and so producing a mirror image (see X:5 and X:6 for further details).

X:1 Branching network pattern

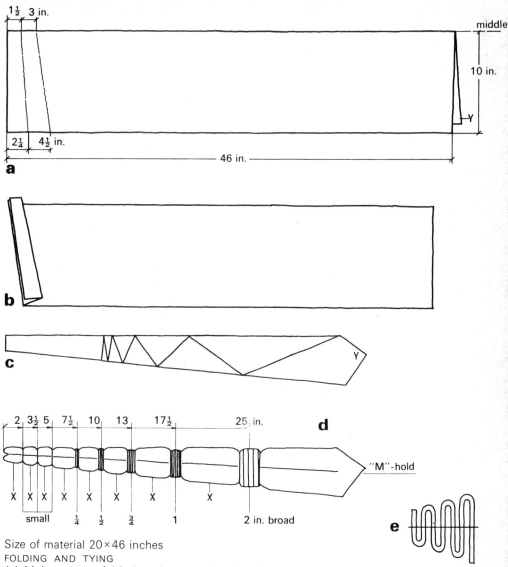

a — 1½ in. · 3 in. · middle · 10 in. · Y · 2¼ · 4½ in. · 46 in.

b

c — Y

d — 2, 3½ 5 · 7½ · 10 · 13 · 17½ · 25 in. · "M"-hold · X X X X X X X X · small · ¼ · ½ · ¾ · 1 · 2 in. broad

e

Size of material 20×46 inches

FOLDING AND TYING

(*a*) Make a center fold, then draw two slanting lines as shown in diagram. (*b*) Fold the material in a pleat along the slanting lines, then fold the rest of the material fan-fashion so that it matches the first pleat. (*c*) If the material is correctly folded then the corner marked Y in diagram (*a*) will reappear at Y in diagram (*c*). (*d*) Bind with string as shown but use a cloth strip for the 25 inch tie. (*e*) Now fold the material expanding concertina-fashion and loosely tie a string around it.

DYEING

After the foundation dyeing, bind on string ties at the points marked X, using a cloth strip for the right-hand one. Make the ties progressively wider. Dip the fabric in the contrast dye. After rinsing the work, remove the eight original ties. Then dip the whole fabric once more in the contrast dye, giving the end with the widest tie the longest time in the dye. See illustration on page 42.

X:2 Triangular branching pattern

Size of material 35 × 50 × 35 inches

A triangular shape is the obvious choice for scarves. The central section covering the crown of the head and the softly draping ends knotted under the chin are very becoming.

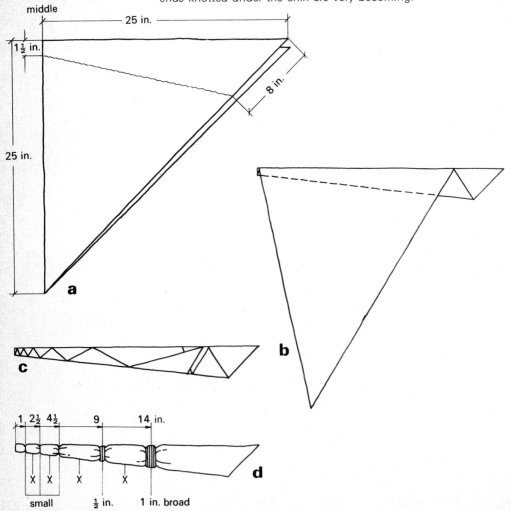

middle

25 in.

$1\frac{1}{2}$ in.

8 in.

25 in.

a

b

c

1 $2\frac{1}{2}$ $4\frac{1}{2}$ 9   14 in.

X X   X   X

small $\frac{1}{2}$ in.   1 in. broad

d

FOLDING AND TYING

(*a*) Fold the material in two and mark a slanting line on the outer surface for the first pleat. (*b*) Lift the slanting line to align with the upper edge of the material. (*c*) Fold the rest of the material fan-fashion to match the first pleat (as in X:1). (*d*) Bind with string ties. (*e*) Fold the material and tie string loosely as in X:1(*e*).

DYEING

After the foundation dyeing, bind with isolating ties at the points marked X. Again, make the tie progressively wider. Grasp the material firmly by the broader end and dip it in the contrast dye until the dye comes $\frac{1}{2}$ inch over the widest tie. Rinse. Remove the five ties first made. Finally, dip the fabric once more to the same depth in the dye, leaving the narrow end in the dye longer than the rest. See illustration on page 42.

X:3 Branching flower pattern

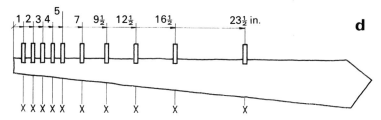

Size of material 20×46 inches

FOLDING AND TYING

(*a*) to (*c*) Fold the material as in X:1 (*a*) to (*c*). (*d*) Clip the pleats together with clothespins (ten in all). (*e*) Fold the material and bind string around as in X:1 (*e*).

DYEING

After the foundation dyeing, place a further ten clothespins at the points marked X. Then dye each of the long sides separately as described in IX:3 on page 66, except that this time the clothespins which were last placed in position must be retained the whole time. See illustration on page 42.

X:4 Pearl necklet pattern

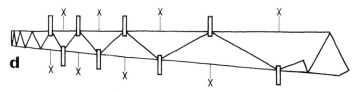

Size of material 20×46 inches

FOLDING AND TYING

(*a*) to (*c*) Fold material as in X:1 (*a*) to (*c*). (*d*) Turn the work over and clothespin the pleats (eight in all). (*e*) Fold material and loosely tie with string as in X:1(*e*).

DYEING

After the foundation dyeing place an additional eight clothespins in position at the points marked X. Then dip the whole fabric in the contrast dye. Rinse. Remove the eight clothespins first placed. Finally, dip the fabric in the dye again, giving the broader end a longer time in the dye. See illustration on page 42.

X:5 Branched lozenge pattern

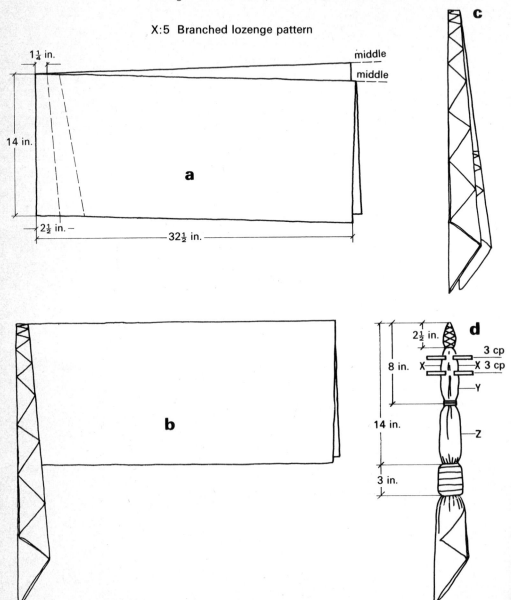

Size of material 28×65 inches

FOLDING AND TYING

(*a*) Make a center fold then fold this in two. Mark out the first pleat by means of two slanting lines on the front. (*b*) Following the slanting lines, make a pleat in the top layers of the cloth only, then pleat the rest of this to match the first pleat. (*c*) Turn the material over and proceed similarly on the other side. (*d*) Grip the top in an M hold and bind on coarse thread in a fairly widely spaced spiral measuring $2\frac{1}{2}$ inches. Place three clothespins on each side at $3\frac{1}{2}$ inch and 5 inch intervals from the top, each clothespin clipping together two pleats. Altogether this will take twelve clothespins. Finally, bind on $\frac{1}{2}$ inch wide isolating string 8 inches from the top, holding the material in an M hold, and similarly bind with a cloth strip 3 inches wide and 14 inches from the top (but this time holding the material in a number of small concertina folds).

DYEING

After the foundation dyeing, place an additional three clothespins on each side at X. Altogether there will now be eighteen clothespins. Make a narrow string tie at Y between the lowest clothespins and the 8 inch tie, and a $1\frac{1}{2}$ inch wide string tie at Z between the cloth strip and the 8 inch tie. Dip the fabric point downward in the contrast dye to a depth of about $17\frac{1}{2}$ inches (that is to about $\frac{1}{2}$ inch above the strip of cloth). After rinsing the work, remove the coarse thread, the first twelve clothespins (leaving six) and the 8 inch tie. Dip the work again point downward to a depth of 13 inches in the contrast dye. Rinse again, and remove the cloth strip. Grip the white band's two outer edges separately in spear holds and dip them to a depth of $1\frac{1}{2}$–2 inches in the dye. Finally, gather all four edges together and dip them in the dye to a depth of $1\frac{1}{2}$–2 inches. See illustration X:6, triple branch pattern on page 42.

X:6 Triple branch pattern and X:7 Double branch pattern

b

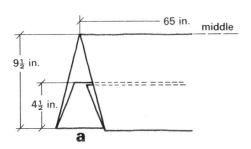

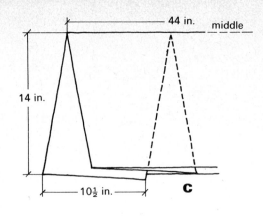

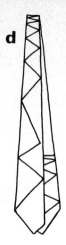

44 in.   middle

14 in.

10½ in.

c

d

Size of material for each pattern 28×65 inches
FOLDING AND TYING
These designs differ only from X:5 in that the sides are folded *before* the material is center folded. For X:6, 4½ inches of each short side is turned in ($\frac{1}{6}$ of breadth, i.e. 27 inches ÷ 6 = 4½ inches) +1 inch at each side. For X:7, 10½ inches of each long side is turned in ($\frac{1}{6}$ of length, i.e. 63 inches ÷ 6 = 10½ inches).
DYEING
This is carried out in the same way as X:5, except that in the case of the triple branch pattern the 4½ inch turned-in edges are dyed instead of the outer edges.

XI Four-cornered designs

These can only be used with square material. They make pretty cushion-covers, head-squares, and table-cloths. The larger the scale in which these are carried out the greater the opportunity for variation, owing to the construction of the pattern.

XI:1 Four-leaf clover pattern

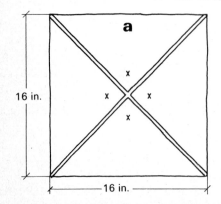

a

x

x   x

x

16 in.

16 in.

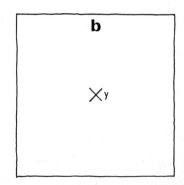

b

X y

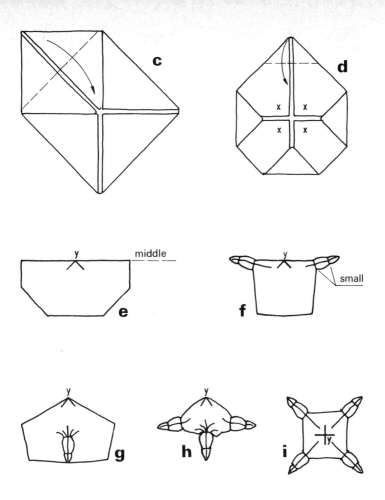

Size of material 23×23 inches

FOLDING AND TYING

(*a*) Make an envelope fold and hold it together with safety-pins at the places marked X. (*b*) Turn the envelope over and mark the middle on the right-hand side at Y. (*c*) Turn the envelope over again, remove the safety-pins and fold once more as an envelope. (*d*) Fold in the corners 2½ inches deep and fasten with safety-pins at the places marked X. (*e*) Fold material in half with the corners inward. (*f*) Grasp the corners along the center fold in an M hold and bind isolating string at 2½ inch and 1 inch intervals from the points. (*g*) Unfold, then fold again, this time at right angles. (*h*) Bind both corners with isolating ties in the same way. (*i*) Remove the safety-pins but try to keep the inner layers undisturbed. Gather material to a point around the center. Spiral bind this for 1½ inches with coarse thread (but not too close together).

73

After the foundation dyeing, dip each of the five tips separately in the contrast dye to the point at which the tie has been made. Rinse, then remove the string binding the four tips and dye each tip separately to the same depth as before. Finally, remove the coarse thread spiral and dip this fifth tip once more in the dye to the same depth. See illustration on page 43.

XI:2 Four-cornered lattice pattern

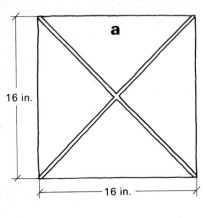

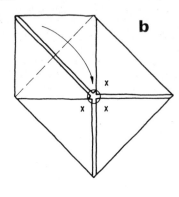

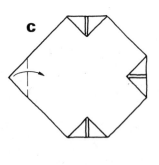

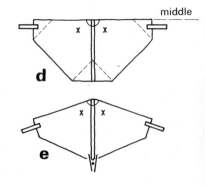

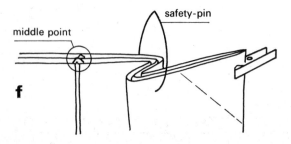

Size of material 23×23 inches

FOLDING AND TYING

(*a*) Make an envelope fold of material. (*b*) Make this into another envelope fold and secure with safety-pins at the places marked X. Mark the center. (*c*) Turn over and fold the corners in 2 inches. (*d*) Fold the material double, with the corners inside. Place a clothespin on each corner ½ inch down from the center fold. (*e*) Open and fold material at right angles to the previous folding and place clothespins on the other two corners in the same way as in (*d*). (*f*) Remove the safety-pins. Clip together each one of the four arms of the "cross" with a clothespin having first arranged them in an S hold as shown in the diagram (to scale). Altogether there are now eight clothespins.

DYEING

After the foundation dyeing, dip each of the four arms of the cross separately in the contrast dye deep enough to cover the two clothespins in each case, holding the material between the clothespins gathered together. Retain this hold while rinsing the fabric, remove the clothespins and dip the same sections again to the same depth in the dye. Finally, fold the fabric with the right-hand side on the outside, gather the fabric together and dip the sides to a depth of 1½ inches in the dye. See illustration on page 43. Note: do not unfold the material immediately: examine it first —it may need a little extra dyeing here and there.

XI:3 Four-cornered leaf pattern

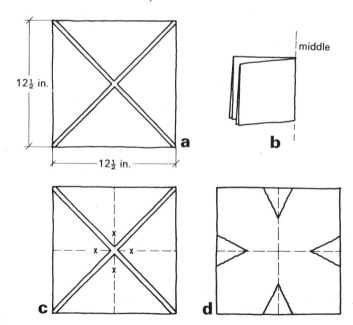

12½ in.

12½ in.

middle

a

b

c

d

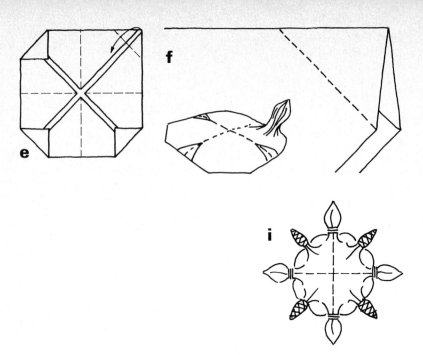

Size of material $17\frac{1}{2} \times 17\frac{1}{2}$ inches

FOLDING AND TYING

(a) Fold the material into an envelope. (b) Fold this envelope into four and crease firmly (this will give guide-lines in the form of a cross). (c) Unfold so that only the original envelope remains. Fasten safety-pins at the points marked X. (d) Turn the work over. Draw four Vs with their points cutting the lines of the cross 3 inches from the edges, and with their two arms touching the edges 3 inches apart. (e) Turn the work over again and fold in 2 inches of the corners. (f) Gather up one of the corners as shown in diagram (to scale) with the front of the envelope facing upward. (g) Make the corner into an M hold and make an isolating tie 2 inches from the tip, using coarse thread to make an X spiral, which should be fairly widely spaced apart. (h) Remove safety-pins. Fold along one of the lines of the cross where a V is drawn. Gather the material along the penciled line and bind around an isolating tie $\frac{1}{2}$ inch wide. (i) Carry out the same procedure with the other three Vs.

DYEING

After the foundation dyeing, dip the four peaks tied with string in the contrast dye until the string ties are covered. Rinse. Remove the string and dip these tips once again to the same depth in the dye. Then remove the coarse thread. Hold the work by the middle of the material and fold it up like an umbrella. Dip the ends in the dye deep enough to leave only 6 inches above the surface to give the fabric a more deeply shaded circular border. See illustration on page 43.

XI:4 Four-cornered pattern

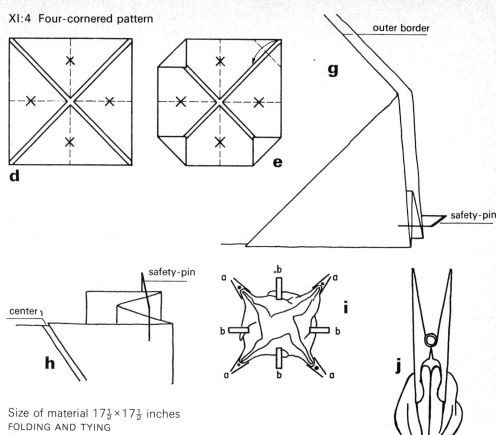

Size of material $17\frac{1}{2} \times 17\frac{1}{2}$ inches

FOLDING AND TYING

(a) to (c) Fold the material and fasten safety-pins as in XI:3 (a) to (c). (d) Draw an X on the cross-lines $2\frac{1}{4}$ inches from the outer edges. (e) Fold the corners in 2 inches from the tips. (f) Gather as in XI:3 (f). (g) Make the corner into an M hold and secure it with a clothespin as in diagram (to scale). Proceed similarly with the other three corners. (h) Turn the work over and remove the safety-pins. Fold the material along one of the cross-lines at X and this will be on the front of the fold. At this point X make the material into an M hold and fasten it together with a clothespin as shown in diagram (j) (actual size). (i) Follow the same procedure with the other sections marked X. Altogether there will now be eight clothespins.

DYEING

After the foundation dyeing, remove the "b" clothespins (see diagram (i)). Then dip the "a" clothespin corners to a depth of about $1\frac{1}{2}$ inches in the contrast dye while the material is gathered together as in diagram (j). After rinsing the work, remove the clothespins and dye the same section again to the same depth. Finally, dip the outer edges in the dye to a depth of about $4\frac{1}{4}$ inches. See illustration on page 43.

77

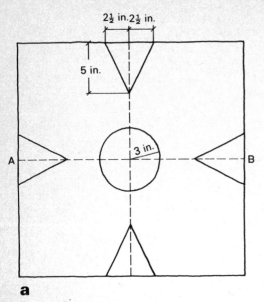

2½ in. 2½ in.

5 in.

3 in.

A ---- B

a

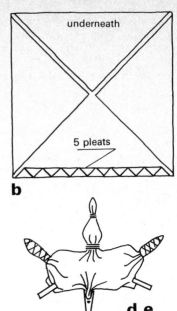

underneath

5 pleats

b

d,e

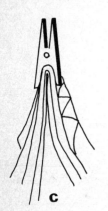

c

Size of material 23×23 inches

FOLDING AND TYING

(*a*) Fold the material into four crease it and then unfold again. Mark the middle and draw a circle with a radius of 3 inches. Draw four Vs as shown in diagram. (*b*) Make an envelope fold. Pleat each of the four triangles as in the diagram. Make each pleat barely ¾ inch wide—there will be five pleats in all. (*c*) Fold each of the four pleated triangles into the middle and secure them with a clothespin. (*d*) Fold the material in half from A to B (see diagram (*a*)) and gather it together where the two Vs lie against one another. Bind the four V-tips spirally with coarse thread for 2½ inches. (*e*) Gather together the material in the center and make a string isolating tie ½ inch in width. Make one more such tie 1½ inches from the tip.

DYEING

After the foundation dyeing, dip each of the parts with a clothespin separately into the contrast dye to a depth of 1 inch. Rinse the work, remove and dip the same section again in the contrast dye. Then dip the middle section to a depth of about 3½ inches in the dye. Remove both string ties and dye the same section again, giving the tip longer in the dye. Remove the coarse thread. Hold the material by the middle and arrange it like an umbrella. Dip the ends until only 9 inches show above the surface of the dye. This will produce a circular darker shade of dye around the outer edges.

XII Cross designs

These designs can be made short or long because the pattern may be repeated *ad infinitum*. Unfortunately, it is not possible to have more than the one pattern in the width, but on the other hand the pattern itself may be enlarged.

XII:1 Circular cross pattern

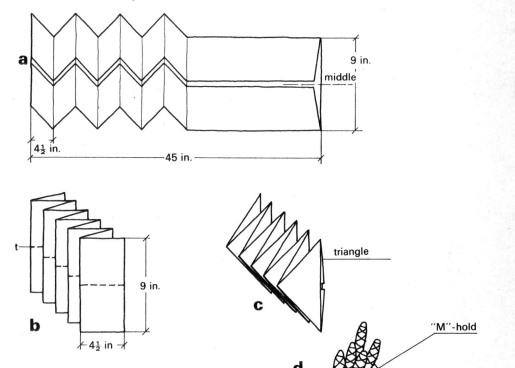

Size of material 18×45 inches

FOLDING AND TYING

(*a*) Fold the material first as a centrally joined fold then concertina-fashion in five pleats, each half-pleat measuring $4\frac{1}{2}$ inches. (*b*) There are now five pleats and the proportions will permit triangular folding—that is, two exact squares. (*c*) Fold each pleat as a triangular fold. (*d*) With coarse thread bind each of the five tips separately in $1\frac{1}{2}$ inch long spirals, then arrange all the ends along each side of the material as indicated in the diagram and bind with string ties $\frac{1}{4}$ inch wide 2 inches in from the tips.

79

After the foundation dyeing, dip the six string-tied ends in the contrast dye so that the string ties are just covered. Rinse. Remove the ties and dip these same tips in the contrast dye to the same depth. Rinse. Dip the five center peaks bound with thread separately in the dye until the thread is covered. Remove the thread and unfold the work. Usually it improves the design to give the outer edges a final 1–1½ inch dip in the dye. See illustration on page 44.

XII:2 Flower cross pattern

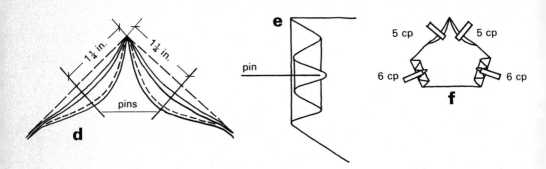

Size of material 18×45 inches

FOLDING AND TYING

(a) to (c) Fold the material as in XII:1 (a) to (c). (d) Clip together each of the five middle points of the triangles separately as in diagram (actual size). There will now be ten clothespins in all. (e) Fold and clothespin together the other sides of each triangle complex, as shown in diagram (actual size). (f) Altogether there will now be twenty-two clothespins.

DYEING

After the foundation dyeing, gather the five middle tips together and dip them in the contrast dye just deep enough to cover the clothespins. Rinse the work and remove the clothespins. There will now be twelve clothespins left altogether. Holding the material gathered together, dip the six folded sections of the one side of the triangle separately in the dye deep enough for the clothespins to be just covered. Rinse the work and remove the clothespins but do *not* unfold the material. Dye these same sections once again. Then treat the six folded sections on the other side of the triangle in the same way. Finally, unfold the material, gather it up and dip the outer edges to a depth of 1–1½ inches in the dye. See illustration on page 44.

XII:3 Peasant flower pattern

Size of material $17\frac{1}{2} \times 22\frac{1}{2}$ inches
This little design is rather special in that it combines the use of both clothespins and isolating string ties and incorporates cross patterning as well as concertina-fold stripes. The design is both charming and individual; the dimensions given are those best suited to it and it is transformed easily into cushion-covers and table-mats. If particularly beautifully executed it also makes an attractive wall-decoration.

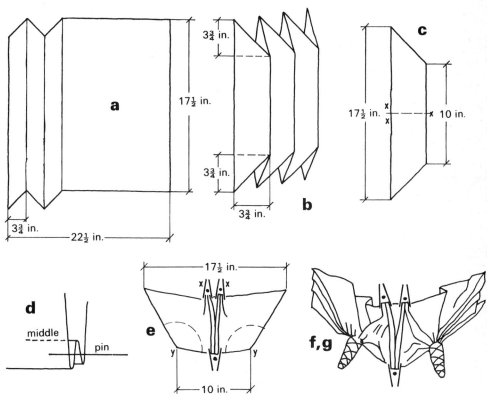

FOLDING AND TYING
(*a*) Fold the material concertina-fashion in three pleats, each half-pleat measuring $3\frac{3}{4}$ inches. (*b*) Make concealed corner folds in each pleat. (*c*) Draw a line across the middle of the work. (*d*) Make an M hold on the 10 inch side along the center line at X (see diagram (*c*)) and keep this in position with a clothespin as in diagram (*d*) (actual size). (*e*) Make M holds on each side of the central line on the $17\frac{1}{2}$ inch length and hold in position with two clothespins at X. (*f*) Fold the corners into M holds at the points marked Y and, using coarse thread, bind a $1\frac{3}{4}$ inch long spiral (not too close together). (*g*) Altogether the material will have three clothespins and two X-spiral points.

After the foundation dyeing, dip the M hold on the 10 inch length in the contrast dye deep enough to cover the clothespin. After rinsing the work, remove the clothespin. Then dip both M holds on the $17\frac{1}{2}$ inch length in the contrast dye deep enough to cover the clothespins. Rinse, and remove *these* clothespins. Then dip each of the thread-tied tips separately in the dye. Rinse, remove the thread and dip the tips once more in the dye to the same depth but giving them a little extra dyeing time. Rinse and unfold the material, fold it again into three concertina folds ($3\frac{3}{4}$ inches to the half-pleat) this time working in the opposite direction. Make two M holds at the same place as before on the $17\frac{1}{2}$ inch length and dip both these into the dye so that the clothespins are completely covered. Finally rinse, and remove clothespins. See illustration on page 44.

XII:4 Flowering creeper pattern

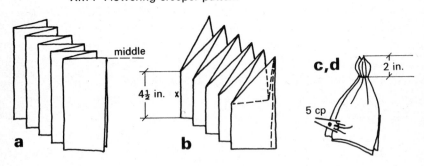

Size of material 18×45 inches

FOLDING AND TYING

(*a*) First make a center fold, then fold concertina-fashion into five pleats, each half-pleat measuring $4\frac{1}{2}$ inches. (*b*) Make the one half of each pleat into a concealed corner fold (note: *the side with the center fold*). (*c*) Make each of the five points into an M hold and bind on an isolating string tie 2 inches from the tip. (*d*) Make M holds on each of the $4\frac{1}{2}$ inch lengths at X and fasten them with five clothespins.

DYEING

After the foundation dyeing, dip the tips in the contrast dye to a depth of $2\frac{1}{2}$ inches. Rinse the material, remove the string and dip the tips once more to an equal depth, giving the outermost edges a little longer dyeing time. Then dip the concertina pleats with the M holds deep enough to cover the clothespins. Rinse and remove the clothespins. Unfold the material and refold into five concertina pleats, each half-pleat measuring $4\frac{1}{2}$ inches, working in the opposite direction. Make a separate M hold for each pleat and fasten with five clothespins as before. Finally, dye the concertina pleats with the M holds in the same way as before.

XIII S-shape designs

The measurements given here are about table-mat size. Numbers
1, 2 and 3 are all easy to execute (an important consideration when
you are making a number of pieces), number 4 is slightly more
complicated. The folding procedure in these designs may also be
carried out on a long narrow cloth with the design running the
other way. In this case the material should be center folded in the
opposite way to that indicated in the diagram, making the S-
shapes much taller and thinner. Numbers 3 and 4 work out well
with larger measurements and make attractive curtains.

XIII:1 River pattern

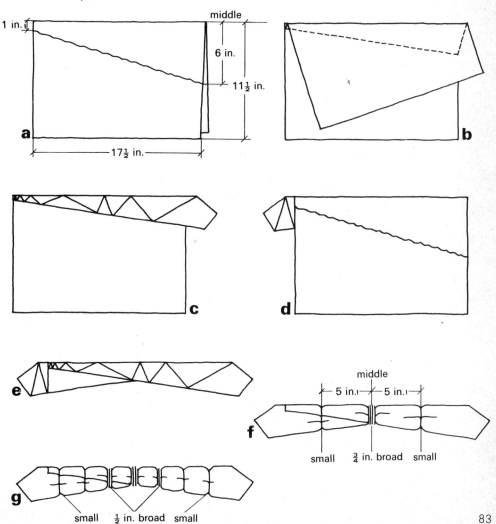

Size of material $17\frac{1}{2} \times 23$ inches

FOLDING AND TYING

(*a*) Make a center fold in the material and mark on the front a slanting line to show where the first pleat will come. (*b*) Place the top layer so that the slanting line lies along the center fold. The dotted line marks the inner pleat. (*c*) Fold the rest of the top layer fan-fashion to match the first pleat. (*d*) Turn the material over and mark out the first pleat in the opposite direction—this produces the S-bend. (*e*) Fold the back of the material in the same way. (*f*) Bind with isolating string. (*g*) Add further ties after the foundation dyeing.

DYEING

After the foundation dyeing attach isolating ties as shown in diagram (*g*). Then fold the material in two, hold the ends and dip the rest in the contrast dye to $\frac{1}{2}$ inch above the outermost ties. Rinse and remove the three ties first placed (the middle tie and the two 5 inch ties). Dip the material once more to the same depth in the dye, giving the middle section a little longer than the rest. Rinse and unfold the material. Finally, dip the short ends in the dye to a depth of about 2 inches, holding the material double and bunched up with the right side on the outside. See illustration on page 44.

XIII:2 Star pattern

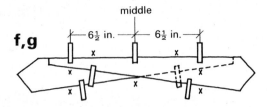

Size of material $17\frac{1}{2} \times 23$ inches

FOLDING AND TYING

(*a*) to (*e*) Fold the material as in XIII:1 (*a*) to (*e*). (*f*) Fasten the pleats with clothespins (seven in all) as in diagram. (*g*) Clip on an additional seven clothespins after the foundation dyeing (facing the first seven clothespins).

DYEING

After the foundation dyeing, clip on the additional seven clothespins, at the points marked X as shown in diagram (*g*). Then fold in two, hold by the ends, and dip in the contrast dye to a depth of $\frac{1}{2}$ inch above the outermost clothespins. Rinse, then remove the seven clothespins first placed. Dip once more in the dye but give the middle section rather longer than the rest. Rinse and unfold. Finally, dip the short ends in the dye to a depth of about 2 inches, holding the material bunched up with right side on the outside. See illustration on page 44.

XIII:3 Double S pattern

Size of material $17\frac{1}{2} \times 23$ inches

FOLDING AND TYING

(a) to (f) Fold and tie the material as in XIII:1 (a) to (f).

DYEING

After the foundation dyeing, remove the ties and unfold the material. Make a center fold as in the diagram on page 83, placing the same side on the outside. Fold the material fan-fashion once more on both sides, working in the opposite direction (i.e. the slanting line marking out the first fold will be drawn 6 inches down from the left-hand side to 1 inch down from the right-hand side). Make three isolating ties again as in XIII:1, then dip the entire fabric in the contrast dye. See illustration on page 44.

XIII:4 Javanese curves

Size of material $17\frac{1}{2} \times 23$ inches

FOLDING AND TYING

(a) to (f) Fold and tie the material as in XIII:2 (a) to (f).

DYEING

After the foundation dyeing, clip on seven additional clothespins at the points marked X as in XIII:2, diagram (g). Next, dip all the pinned edges to a depth of about $\frac{1}{4}$ inch in the contrast dye, holding the material together in concertina folds. Rinse, remove the clothespins and unfold the material. Once again make a center fold as in XIII:1, diagram (a), with the same side to the outside. Fold both sides once more in fan pleats, working in the opposite direction (i.e. the slanting line marking out the first fold should be drawn 6 inches down from the left-hand side to 1 inch down from the right-hand side). Clothespins are used this time as well. Finally, dip the pinned edges in the contrast dye to a depth of about $\frac{1}{4}$ inch, holding the material in concertina folds. See illustration on page 44.

Three-color dye designs

Tie-dyeing gives great scope for expressing yourself in color. A fabric tie-dyed in one color can look tame beside a multicolor one, and the work itself is more interesting if several dyes are used. Also, it is not necessarily more time-consuming. With a little practice small amounts of concentrated dye solutions can be speedily made up, and dyeing times are usually short.

The following notes are intended as a guide to using three colors in the designs outlined in the basic design section. In each case the material is folded in the same way as it is for two-dye patterns. For the sake of simplicity we have used the same three colors throughout: turquoise for the foundation dye, yellow and violet for the contrast dyes. Instructions for rinsing and other basic procedures are also as those given in the basic design section. Notes on tying and dyeing have only been included where they differ from the two-color procedure. The illustrations on pages 35, 36, 38, 41, 42, 43 and 44 show examples of three-dye designs.

I Stripes

I:1 Radar waves and I:2 Rocket glow
Fold and bind as in two-dye instructions I:1 (*a*) to (*b*) on page 27. Foundation dye in turquoise. Remove 4 inch ties. Dip to about $4\frac{1}{2}$ inches in the yellow dye. Remove 2 inch ties. Dip in the violet dye to about 3 inches.

I:3 Water reflections
Fold and bind as in two-dye instructions I:2 (*a*) to (*b*) on page 27. Foundation dye in turquoise. Remove 5 inch clothespins. Dip to about $5\frac{1}{2}$ inches in the yellow dye. Remove $2\frac{1}{2}$ inch clothespins. Dip in the violet dye to about $3\frac{1}{2}$ inches.

I:4 Center-line pattern
Fold and bind as in two-dye instructions I:4 (*a*) to (*b*) on page 28. Foundation dye in turquoise. Remove 3 inch tie. Dip the end with the white band about $3\frac{1}{2}$ inches in the yellow dye. Remove the 1 inch tie. Dip this same end to about $1\frac{1}{2}$ inches in the violet dye.

I:5 Ladder pattern
Fold and bind as in two-dye instructions I:5 (*a*) to (*b*) on page 28. Foundation dye in turquoise. Remove the 2 inch clothespins. Dip the end with the two clothespins in the violet dye for about $2\frac{1}{2}$ inches. Remove the last two clothespins. Dip the same end in the yellow dye to a depth of about $1\frac{1}{2}$ inches.

I:6 Side lines

Fold and bind as in two-dye instructions I:6 (*a*) to (*b*) on page 29. Foundation dye in turquoise. Bind isolating string to a width of $\frac{1}{2}$ inch around middle. Remove the $\frac{1}{2}$ inch ties and dip the whole fabric in the violet dye. Remove $2\frac{1}{4}$ inch ties and dip middle section in the yellow dye so that only about $1\frac{3}{4}$ inches of the ends show above the surface of the dye.

I:7 Flower stripes

Fold and bind as in two-dye instructions I:7 (*a*) to (*b*) on page 29. Foundation dye in turquoise. Dip both ends about 1 inch in the violet dye. Remove clothespins. Dip two of the corners diagonally opposed to one another in the violet dye and the other two in the yellow dye, holding the tips bunched together.

I:8 Floral border (A)

Fold and bind as in two-dye instructions I:8 (*a*) to (*d*) on page 30. Foundation dye in turquoise. Place the four clothespins and remove both $2\frac{3}{4}$ inch ties. Dip the ends some $3\frac{1}{4}$ inches in the violet dye giving the deepest color to the clothespin section. Remove both $1\frac{1}{4}$ inch ties and dip ends some $1\frac{1}{2}$ inches in the yellow dye.

I:9 Floral borders (B)

Fold and bind as in the two-dye instructions I:9 (*a*) to (*c*) on page 31. Foundation dye in turquoise. Place eight clothespins as in (*d*) on page 31. Remove ties. Dip the ends for some $3\frac{1}{2}$ inches in the violet dye, leaving $\frac{1}{2}$ inch of the outer edges longer in the dye. Remove the four clothespins first placed (the corner clothespins). Dip the four corners separately about 1 inch in the yellow dye, holding the tips gathered together.

I:10 Floral border (C)

Fold and bind as in two-dye instructions 1:10 (*a*) to (*c*) on page 31. Foundation dye in turquoise. Place the eight clothespins as in (d). Dip the whole fabric in the violet dye. Remove both ties and dip the middle part in the yellow dye so that only $1\frac{3}{4}$ inches of the ends remain above the dye. Remove cloth strip and dip sides of the middle section in the violet dye for some $1\frac{3}{4}$ inches, having first made them into a spear hold.

I:11 Creeper pattern

Size of material approximately 15×35 inches

This design is not described in the two-dye instructions. Center-fold the material along its length and make five concertina folds with each half-pleat measuring $3\frac{1}{2}$ inches. Place a clothespin in the middle of the short end along the center-fold line. Dip the material, other end first, in the turquoise dye leaving about $1\frac{1}{2}$ inches above the clothespin clear of the dye. Remove the clothespin and dip about 1 inch of this side in the contrast dye. Dye half of the long sides (nearest the center fold) each separately in another contrast dye, holding them in a spear hold. Unfold the concertina folds, refold in reverse and repeat dyeing as above. Finally, make an M hold of the outer edges and dip for some $1-1\frac{1}{2}$ inches in the contrast dye. See illustration on page 34.

II Checks

II:1 Flowered checks

Fold and bind the dye as in the two-dye instructions on page 32. Unfold material and fold concertina-fashion so that the folds come in the middle of the white streaks (four pleats in all). Make sure that the right side of the material is uppermost. Fold concertina-fashion so that there are three pleats, each half-pleat measuring $2\frac{1}{2}$ inches. Dip the short end, where there are no edges, in the yellow dye for about $\frac{3}{4}$ inch, holding the material in an M hold.

II:2 Crystal checks (A)

Dye according to the two-dye instructions on page 45 and unfold the material. Then bunch it together as described in VI:1 (A) on page 56 and dip the middle section only about 1 inch in the yellow dye.

II:2 Crystal checks (B)

Dye as in the two-dye instructions in II:2 on page 45 and unfold the material. Then fold in half with the right side facing upward (it now measures $17\frac{1}{2} \times 11\frac{1}{4}$ inches). Fold the material fan-fashion as described in IX:1 on page 65. Make a pleat $\frac{3}{4}$ inch wide on the folded long side and $2\frac{1}{2}$ inches wide on the other. Fan-pleat in expanding concertina-fashion and dip only the outermost edges of the long sides of the material in the yellow dye.

II:3 Feathery checks

Dye as in the two-dye instructions on page 46 and unfold the material. Then fold again along its length in two simple concertina folds, right side facing outermost. Then fold it into six concertina folds (following the lines). Dip the short sides, where the outer edges of the material show, about 1 inch in the yellow dye. Unfold the concertina pleats and dip both the short sides 1 inch in the yellow dye.

II:4 Four-cornered flower checks

First carry out all the dyeing procedure exactly as described in the two-dye instructions on page 46. Remove the six remaining clothespins and dip all the corner tips with white spots about 1 inch in the yellow dye, holding them bunched together to make a fine veining of yellow.

II:5 Butterfly checks

Dye the material according to the two-dye instructions on page 47. Unfold the concertina pleats and refold again in the other direction. Dip the pinned sides about 1 inch in the yellow dye, holding the material in an M hold.

II:6 Checked garland

First dip in the violet dye as described in the two-dye instructions on page 47. Unfold the concertina pleats and refold in the opposite direction. Dip all the corners 1 inch in the yellow dye, holding them bunched together to make a fine yellow veining.

II:7 Star burst pattern
Size of material approximately 20×40 inches
This design is not described in the basic designs section. It is quick to execute, the folding is simple, no ties are needed and the "stars" are easy to dye.

First make a center fold lengthwise then a centrally joined fold. Fold the material concertina-fashion in three pleats (it will then measure 5×5 inches). Gather up the points in one of the corners, holding the middle of the material in the other hand. Dip the corner 2 inches in a contrast dye, say, mustard-yellow. Then dip $\frac{1}{2}$ inch of the tips in the turquoise dye. Repeat with the opposite corner using a different color, say, violet, with $\frac{1}{2}$ inch green tips. Unfold, refold in the opposite direction in concertina pleats and repeat the dyeing procedure on these corners. In the same way dip the two remaining corners in a turquoise contrast dye. Unfold and dip all the outer edges for $1\frac{1}{2}$–2 inches in the turquoise dye. See illustration on page 35.

III Squares
III:1 Basic square (A)
Fold and tie as in the two-dye instructions (a) to (b) on page 48. Foundation dye in turquoise. Tie a string for one turn only midway between the $5\frac{1}{2}$ inch and $8\frac{1}{2}$ inch ties and remove the $8\frac{1}{2}$ inch tie. Place a 1 inch wide string tie some 3–4 inches from the top. Hold the material by the point and dip in the violet dye so that only $3\frac{1}{2}$ inches remain above the surface of the dye. Remove the $5\frac{1}{2}$ inch tie and dip the top $6\frac{1}{2}$ inches in the yellow dye.

III:1 Basic square (B)
Fold, tie and dye according to the two-dye instructions on page 48 and leave the tie at X in position. Dip the gathered tip about 3 inches in the yellow dye. Remove the string and smooth out the triangle. Mark out a point $6\frac{1}{2}$ inches along the 23 inch side and draw a straight, perpendicular line. Gather the material along the line and dip the end in the yellow dye as far as the gathering. Dye the opposite end in the same way.

III:2 Four-cornered tower
Fold, tie and dye according to the two-dye instructions on page 49, leaving the four clothespins in position. Hold the material gathered together in straight gathers 3 inches from the tip and dip in the yellow dye to the point at which it is held. Remove both clothespins from the one side. Hold the material in a spear hold at the point marked by the white dots and dip to a depth of $\frac{3}{4}$–1 inch in the yellow dye. Proceed in the same way with the other side.

III:3 Flower square
Fold and tie as in two-dye instructions (a) to (d) on pages 49–50. Foundation dye in turquoise. Dip the tip in the violet dye until the string tie is covered. Remove the string tie and the coarse thread tie and dip the same section in the violet dye once more,

giving the tip a little extra time in the dye. Straighten the folds by the clothespins and dip each side separately in the violet dye. Hold the material gathered together immediately below the clothespins and dip so that these are just covered. Remove the clothespins but keep the material gathered as before and dip the same sections again, this time in the yellow dye. Finally, dip the bunched edges about 1 inch in the violet dye.

IV Rectangles

IV:1 Basic rectangle
Fold and tie the material as in the two-dye instructions (a) to (d) on page 50. Foundation dye in turquoise. Tie string for one turn only midway between the $4\frac{1}{2}$ inch and the $1\frac{3}{4}$ inch ties and remove the $1\frac{3}{4}$ inch tie. Bind about 2 inches of the tip with coarse thread at the center fold in a well-spaced-out spiral. Dip the whole fabric in the violet dye, giving the outer edges a little extra dyeing time. Remove the coarse thread and the $9\frac{1}{2}$ inch tie and dip the tip up to the string tie in the yellow dye.

IV:2 Rectangular tower
Fold, tie and dye the material as in the two-dye instructions on page 51, keeping the twelve clothespins in position. Gather the material midway between the center fold and the clothespins and bind on a $\frac{1}{2}$ inch wide isolating string. Remove clothespins and dip the tip in the yellow dye deep enough for the white dots to be completely covered.

V Circles

V:1 Basic circle
Fold, tie and dye according to the two-dye instructions on page 52. Remove the 5 inch tie and the coarse thread. Bind the tip with coarse thread in an X spiral but this time to a depth of 3 inches only. Dip this tip to a depth of $5\frac{1}{2}$ inches in the yellow dye.

V:2 Three-circle pattern
Fold and tie as in the two-dye instructions (a) to (c) on page 53. Foundation dye in turqoise. Bind the three tips with coarse thread in an X spiral and remove the 4 inch and the $5\frac{1}{2}$ inch ties. Dip the material tip first in the violet dye deep enough to submerge the string holding it together $\frac{1}{2}$ inch under the surface of the dye. Give the tips a little extra dyeing time. Remove the coarse thread and bind the tips in a well-spaced X spiral but this time to a depth of only $1\frac{1}{2}$ inches. Remove the $2\frac{1}{2}$ inch tie. Dip material, tips first, 3 inches in the yellow dye.

V:3 Sun pattern
Fold, tie and dye according to the two-dye instructions on page 54. Remove the 5 inch tie and the coarse thread. Bind the top with coarse thread in a spiral but this time for only 3 inches. Dip the top to a depth of $5\frac{1}{2}$ inches in the yellow dye.

V:4 Sunbeam pattern
Fold and tie according to the two-dye instructions (a) to (e)

on page 55. Foundation dye in turquoise. Clip on a clothespin at X. Gather the material between the tip and the $5\frac{1}{2}$ inch clothespins and bind it with a string tie $\frac{1}{2}$ inch wide. Remove the $8\frac{1}{2}$ inch clothespins. Eight clothespins are now left altogether. Hold the work by the point and dip it outer edges foremost in the violet dye to cover the $5\frac{1}{2}$ inch clothespins completely, giving the outer edges a little extra dyeing. Remove the $5\frac{1}{2}$ inch clothespins. Finally, dip the tip about 6–$6\frac{1}{2}$ inches in the yellow dye.

VI Ovals

VI:1 Basic oval
Fold and tie according to the two-dye instructions in (a) to (d) on page 56. Foundation dye in turquoise. Bind, for one turn only, a third string tie midway between the $3\frac{1}{2}$ inch and the 6 inch ties. Gather the tip and bind it with coarse thread in an X spiral for 3 inches at fairly widely spaced intervals. Dip the entire fabric in the violet dye. Remove the coarse thread and rebind the top in an X spiral but this time to a depth of 2 inches only. Remove the $3\frac{1}{2}$ inch tie. Finally, dip the top about 4–$4\frac{1}{2}$ inches in the yellow dye.

VI:2 Stadium design
Fold and tie according to the two-dye instructions (a) to (j) on pages 57–58. Foundation dye in turquoise. Clip on an additional six clothespins between the 2 inch and the 4 inch clothespins at X. Then remove the six 2 inch clothespins. Gather the material between the 4 inch clothespins and the center fold and bind the tip with coarse thread in a widely spaced spiral for $3\frac{1}{2}$ inches. Dip the whole material in the violet dye. Remove the coarse thread and rebind tip in a widely spaced spiral but this time for only 2–$2\frac{1}{2}$ inches. Remove the 4 inch clothespins and dip the tip for about $4\frac{1}{2}$ inches in the yellow dye.

VI:3 Oval flower design
Fold and tie according to the two-dye instructions in (a) to (j) on page 58. Foundation dye in turquoise. Bind with isolating string to a width of $\frac{1}{2}$ inch between the cloth strip and the clothes-pins. Dip the whole fabric in the yellow dye. Remove the cloth strip and dip the tip up to the string tie in the violet dye. Remove the clothespin at the tip and dip the latter to a depth of 1 inch in the yellow dye. Remove the string tie. Remove the two 3 inch clothespins along the one side. Hold the material in a spear hold where the white dots appear and dip to a depth of 1 inch in the violet dye. Proceed similarly on the other side. See illustration on page 38.

VII Diagonal designs

VII:1 Basic diagonal design
Fold and tie according to the two-dye instructions (a) to (e) on page 59. Place an isolating tie between the $1\frac{1}{2}$ inch and the 4 inch ties. Foundation dye in turquoise. Bind a string tie for one turn only midway between the 6 inch and the 10 inch ties and another one

between the 10 inch tie and the further end. Remove the 1½ inch tie and dip this end 3–3½ inches in the violet dye. Dip the other end to a depth of about 2½ inches in the violet dye. Remove the string tie between the 1½ inch, the 4 inch and the 10 inch ties. Hold the material by both ends and dip in the yellow dye leaving only 1 inch of the ends uncovered. Remove the cloth strip and, holding in a spear hold, dye both the long sides separately in the violet dye at the point of the 2 inch band. Unfold the concertina pleats and refold in the opposite direction. Repeat the violet dyeing of the white band as above.

VII:2 Diagonal flower pattern

Fold and tie according to the two-dye instructions (a) to (e) on page 60. Foundation dye in turquoise and fasten a further twelve clothespins on the central section, three at each of the points marked X. Then dip the central part in the violet dye submerging everything except 3½ inches of the ends. Remove the eighteen clothespins first clipped on the central section. Twenty-four clothespins are now left. Dip the central section in the yellow dye leaving only 3 inches of the ends uncovered. Remove all the rest of the clothespins and dip each of the four corners separately to a depth of about 1 inch in the violet dye, keeping the tips gathered together.

VII:3 Diagonal square pattern

Fold and tie according to the two-dye instructions in (a) to (c) on page 60. Foundation dye in turquoise. Bind on additional string ties at X and remove both the 1¼ inch ties. Dip the whole work in the violet dye. Remove the 4 inch tie. Hold the material by both ends and dip the middle section in the yellow dye so that only 1½ inches remain uncovered.

VII:4 Square flower pattern

Fold and tie as in the two-dye instructions in (a) to (d) on page 61. Foundation dye in turquoise. Remove the eighteen corner clothespins and fasten a further twenty-seven clothespins on the central section as shown in diagram (e) on page 60. Dip the whole fabric in the violet dye. Remove the nine clothespins placed on the middle section. Hold the fabric at both ends and dip the middle section in the yellow dye so that only 2½–3 inches remain uncovered.

VIII Herringbone designs

VIII:1 Feather pattern

Fold, tie and dye as in the two-dye instructions on page 62. Unfold the concertina pleating (but retain the zigzag folds) and repleat the concertina folds in the opposite direction. Make an M hold in the material as before and dip the opposite long side to a depth of 1–1½ inches in the yellow dye. The outermost edges should be given a little extra dyeing time.

VIII:2 VX design

Fold, tie and dye as in the two-dye instructions on page 62. Unfold the concertina and zigzag folds but retain the center fold.

Refold concertina and zigzag folds, this time working in the opposite direction. Bind a string tie around the middle green band. Dip the end of the material in the yellow dye as far as the midway point on the tie, giving the outer section a little extra dyeing time.

VIII:3 Zigzag leaves

Fold, tie and dye as in the two-dye instructions on page 62. Unfold the concertina and the zigzag folds (but retain the center fold). Refold the concertina and zigzag folds working in the opposite direction. Bind a string tie around the ends $\frac{1}{2}$ inch in from the edge (over the green stripes). Finally, dip first the one and then the other end to a depth of 2 inches in the yellow dye, giving the outer edges a little extra dyeing time.

VIII:4 Flower pattern

Fold, tie and dye according to the two-dye instructions on page 63. Remove the twelve remaining clothespins. Hold the material by both ends and dip the central section in the yellow dye as far as the violet dots so that these are given just a few decorative yellow veins.

VIII:5 Double herringbone pattern (A)

Fold, tie and dye as in the two-dye instructions on page 63. Unfold the concertina and zigzag folds (retaining the center fold and centrally joined fold). Refold the concertina and zigzag folds working in the opposite direction. Hold material firmly in the middle and dip the four sides to a depth of $\frac{1}{4}-\frac{1}{2}$ inch in the yellow dye.

VIII:5 Double herringbone pattern (B)

Fold, tie and dye as in the two-dye instructions on page 63. Unfold the concertina fold only (not the zigzag one) and refold again in the opposite direction. Dip the two lightly colored sides in the violet dye to a depth of $\frac{1}{4}-\frac{1}{2}$ inch. Unfold the concertina and zigzag folds, refold in the opposite direction. Hold material firmly by the middle section and dip the four sides to a depth of $\frac{1}{4}-\frac{1}{2}$ inch in the yellow dye. Unfold the concertina (but not the zigzag) folds and refold in the opposite direction. Dip both the sides that have not been given a yellow color to a depth of $\frac{1}{4}-\frac{1}{2}$ inch in the yellow dye.

IX Fan-shape designs

IX:1 Basic fan pattern

Fold and tie as in the two-dye instructions (*a*) to (*e*) on page 65. Foundation dye in turquoise. Bind with isolating ties of string and a strip of cloth at the points marked X, again progressively increasing the width of the ties. Remove the $2\frac{1}{2}$ inch, 10 inch, $19\frac{1}{2}$ inch and $34\frac{1}{2}$ inch ties. Dip the fabric in the violet dye giving a little extra dyeing time to the wider of the borders. Bind string ties on the four violet stripes and the tinted zones below these as far as the next tie. Remove the 4 inch, 6 inch, 12 inch, 14 inch, $22\frac{1}{2}$ inch, 26 inch and $37\frac{1}{2}$ inch ties. Dip the whole fabric in the yellow dye.

IX:2 Dotted ray pattern

Fold and tie as in the two-dye instructions (*a*) to (*e*) on page 65. Foundation dye in turquoise. Clip on seven clothespins at the points marked X and remove the 3 inch, $9\frac{1}{2}$ inch, 20 inch and 35 inch clothespins, leaving ten clothespins altogether. Dip the whole fabric in the violet dye giving a little extra time to the wider end. Remove all clothespins but do not unfold the fan pleating. The white dots left by the clothespins now receive a yellow dyeing. Fold the material in half along the line of the 6 inch dots and dip in the dye just far enough to leave the green dots above the level of the dye. Proceed similarly with the 14 inch and $27\frac{1}{2}$ inch dots.

IX:3 Peacock pattern

Fold and tie as in the two-dye instructions (*a*) to (*f*) on pages 65–66. Foundation dye in turquoise. Clip on an additional seven clothespins at the points marked X and remove the 3 inch, 10 inch, 20 inch and $39\frac{1}{2}$ inch clothespins. Ten clothespins will now be left. Fold the material according to IX:3 (*f*) but this time keeping the pinned side quite flat. Then dip this flat side, with the clothespins, to a depth of $\frac{1}{2}$ inch in the violet dye. Unfold the concertina pleats and remove the clothespins. The areas around the white dots, where 6 inch, $14\frac{1}{2}$ inch and $28\frac{1}{2}$ inch clothespins were placed, must now be dyed yellow. First fold the material in two along the line of the 6 inch dots and dip in the contrast dye so that the green dots just clear the dye surface. Proceed similarly along the lines of the $14\frac{1}{2}$ inch and $28\frac{1}{2}$ inch dots.

IX:4 Eye pattern

Fold and tie as in the two-dye instructions (*a*) to (*d*) on page 66. Foundation dye in turquoise. Bind a $\frac{1}{2}$ inch wide tie at Y and put a further twelve clothespins at the points marked X. Altogether there will now be eighteen clothespins. Dip the fabric tip foremost in the violet dye to a depth of 8 inches. Remove the six clothespins in the center and repeat the violet dyeing procedure. Remove the coarse thread and dip the tip about $3\frac{1}{2}$ inches in the yellow dye. Remove the $9\frac{1}{2}$ inch tie. Dip the work in the dye with the two short ends foremost just deep enough to cover the white band made by the string tie. Remove the cloth strip, make each white edge into a separate spear hold and dip them to a depth of 1 inch in the violet dye. See illustration on page 41.

X Branching designs
X:1 Branching network pattern

Fold and tie as in the two-dye instructions (*a*) to (*e*) on pages 67–68. Foundation dye in turquoise. Bind on isolating ties and a cloth strip at the points marked X, progressively increasing the width of the ties. Remove the $3\frac{1}{2}$ inch, $7\frac{1}{2}$ inch, 13 inch and 25 inch ties. Dip the fabric in the violet dye, giving the widest part a little extra dyeing time. Bind with isolating ties around the four violet stripes and the four tinted stripes above these. Remove the 2 inch, 5 inch, 10 inch and $17\frac{1}{2}$ inch ties. Dip the whole fabric in the yellow dye.

X:2 Triangular branching pattern

Fold and tie as in the two-dye instructions (*a*) to (*e*) on page 69. Foundation dye in turquoise. Bind with isolating ties at the points marked X, progressively increasing the width of the ties. Remove the 1 inch, $4\frac{1}{2}$ inch and 14 inch ties. Hold the material by the wider end and dip in the violet dye to $\frac{1}{2}$ inch above the widest isolating tie. Bind isolating ties around the three violet stripes and the three tinted stripes above these, in the direction in which the material narrows, and up to the next tie. Remove the $2\frac{1}{2}$ inch and 9 inch isolating ties. Dip the tip in the yellow dye to a depth of $11\frac{1}{2}$ inches.

X:3 Branching flower pattern

Fold and tie as in the two-dye instructions (*a*) to (*e*) on page 69. Foundation dye in turquoise. Clip on ten clothespins at the points marked X and remove the clothespins clipped on before dyeing at 1 inch, 3 inch, 5 inch, $9\frac{1}{2}$ inch and $16\frac{1}{2}$ inch intervals. This will leave fifteen clothespins. Fold the material expanding concertina-fashion keeping one of the sides flat (see IX:3 (*f*) on page 65). Dip the flat side to a depth of $\frac{1}{2}$ inch in the violet dye. Refold once more as in (*f*) but this time so that the other side is left flat. Dye this also in the violet dye. Remove all the clothespins but retain the system of folds needed to produce a branch design. The white dots made by the clothespins must be dyed yellow. Fold the material in half along the line of the 1 inch dots and dip in the dye up to but not over the violet dots on either side. Then dye all the other white dots in the same way, giving progressively more dyeing time as the distance between the dots increases.

X:4 Pearl necklet pattern

Fold and tie as in the two-dye instructions (*a*) to (*e*) on pages 69–70. Foundation dye in turquoise. Clip on an extra eight clothespins at the points marked X and remove the clothespins first placed along the long side. Altogether there will now be twelve clothespins. Dip the fabric completely in the violet dye giving the wider end a little extra dyeing time. Then remove all the clothespins but retain the folding needed for the branched design. The areas where the clothespins made a pattern of white dots must now be dyed yellow. Begin by folding the material into two along the narrow side and dipping it in the dye so that the violet dots on either side are well above the dye. Next, dye all the other white dots in a similar fashion, giving progressively more dyeing time as the distance between the dots increases.

X:5 Branched lozenge pattern

Fold and tie as in the two-dye instructions (*a*) to (*d*) on page 70. Foundation dye in turquoise. Clip an additional three clothespins on to each side at the points marked X. Bind on a narrow isolating string tie midway between the 8 inch tie and the clothespins nearest Y and also a $1\frac{1}{2}$ inch tie between the 8 inch tie and the cloth strip at Z. Dip the fabric tip foremost in the violet dye to a depth of 13 inches (that is, $\frac{1}{2}$ inch above the cloth strip). Remove the twelve clothespins first placed and the 8 inch tie. Then, tip foremost, dip the material in the violet dye up to a depth of 13 inches.

Note: replace the twelve clothespins over the violet dots and re-move the six from the central section and the coarse thread tie. Dip the tip in the yellow dye up to the tie nearest the clothespins. Make a spear hold of the outer edge of the white band and dip about $1\frac{1}{2}$–2 inches in the yellow dye. Make another spear hold of the other outer edge and dye in the violet dye. Finally, dip all four edges to a depth of $1\frac{1}{2}$–2 inches in the violet or yellow dye while holding the material bunched up together.

X:6 Triple branch pattern
This design differs from X:5 above in the folding only which is here carried out lengthwise. The rest of the procedure is similar except ultimately the long sides are dyed violet along the $4\frac{1}{2}$ inch folds and the outer margins are dyed in yellow. See illustration on page 42.

XI Four-cornered designs
XI:1 Four-leaf clover pattern
Fold and tie as in the two-dye instructions (a) to (i) on page 73. Foundation dye in turquoise. Dip each of the four string-tied tips separately in the violet dye until the tie is covered. Remove the ties and dip them separately once again in the violet dye to the same depth. Dip the tip bound with coarse thread in the violet dye to a depth of $1\frac{3}{4}$ inches. Remove the coarse thread and dip the tip $\frac{3}{4}$ inch in the yellow dye. Unfold the fabric to the point until it resumes the shape of a double envelope. It should now measure 12×12 inches. Dip each of the four corners separately to a depth of $1\frac{1}{2}$–2 inches in the yellow dye while holding the material bunched up together.

XI:2 Four-cornered lattice pattern
Fold and tie as in the two-dye instructions (a) to (f) on page 75. Foundation dye in turquoise. Dip one of the four arms of the cross in the violet dye just deep enough to cover both the clothespins. The material between the clothespins should be held gathered together. Remove the clothespin with the S hold but retain the S hold itself and dip the same section in the violet dye once more to the same depth. Proceed similarly with the other three arms of the cross. Next remove one of the outer clothespins holding the cross but do not alter the folding. Dip the right-angled corner in the yellow dye to a depth of about $1\frac{1}{2}$ inches keeping the material gathered together. Proceed similarly with the other three corners. Unfold the material, then fold in half with the right side on the outside and dip the edges (which should be kept gathered together) to a depth of about $1\frac{1}{2}$ inches in the violet dye.

XI:3 Four-cornered leaf pattern
Fold and tie as in the two-dye instructions (a) to (i) on page 76. Foundation dye in turquoise. Dip the four string-tied tips in the violet dye deep enough to cover the ties. Remove the string ties and dip these same tips once more in the yellow dye to the same depth. Remove the coarse thread and unfold. Grip the material by the center folding it up like an umbrella and dip the ends so that only 6 inches remain uncovered. By this means a circular, more deeply shaded pattern is produced at the outer edges of the fabric.

XI:4 Four-cornered pattern

Fold and tie as in the two-dye instructions (a) to (i) on page 77 Foundation dye in turquoise. Remove one of the "b" clothespins but keep the fold intact and dip the corner $\frac{3}{4}$–1 inch in the yellow dye, keeping it gathered together the while. Proceed in the same way with the other three "b" clothespins. Next, dip each of the four "a" clothespin corners separately to a depth of $1\frac{1}{2}$ inches in the violet dye holding the material as in XI:4 (j) on page 77. Remove the clothespins and once more dip the same sections to the same depth in the violet dye. Finally, dip the gathered-up outer edges about 1 inch in the violet dye.

XI:5 Four-cornered flower pattern

Fold and tie as in the two-dye instructions (a) to (e) on page 78. Foundation dye in turquoise. Gather the material by the clothes-pins, each one separately, and dip in the violet dye far enough to cover the clothespins. Remove one of the clothespins, keeping the material folded, and dip one of the corners in the yellow dye as far as the violet dye was dipped. Do likewise with the other three corners. Remove the coarse thread from the four corner tips and dip in the violet dye far enough to cover the white stripes. Unfold, refold like an umbrella and then dip the outer edges in the yellow dye until only $9\frac{1}{2}$ inches remain above the dye. This gives the fabric a circular shaded effect at the outer edges. See illustration on page 43.

XI:6 Four-cornered wreath pattern

Size of material 23×23 inches

This design is not included in the two-dye instructions. (a) Make an envelope fold of fabric. (b) Make this into a further envelope fold and draw a cross on the smooth side to divide the folded material into four quarters. (c) Draw a triangle at each of the outer edges which will cut the center-line $3\frac{1}{2}$ inches in, extending to $1\frac{1}{2}$ inches on each side of this line. (d) Fold the material in two so that the drawing comes on the outside and gather it together at the center fold along one of the penciled lines. Tie string around this and proceed in the same way with the other three sides. (e) Turn in the four corners 2 inches as described in XI:2. Fold them again and clip clothespins in position as described in XI:2 (d) on page 75.

DYEING

Dye the four corners with the clothespins in turquoise, then dip the four with string ties in the violet dye so that the ties are just covered. Remove one of the ties but keep the material folded and dip it in the yellow dye so that the white stripe is just covered. Remove the three other string ties and dye the rest of the fabric in a similar fashion. Finally, remove one of the clothespins and dip the corner in the violet dye just deep enough to cover the white dots. Follow the same dyeing procedure with the other three clothespins. See illustration on page 43.

XII Cross designs

XII:1 Circular cross pattern

Fold and tie as in the two-dye instructions (a) to (d) on page 79. Foundation dye in turquoise. Dip each of the six tips bound with string ties separately in the violet dye just far enough to cover the tie. Remove the ties and dip the same tips to the same depth in the yellow dye. Dip each of the five points bound with coarse thread separately in the violet dye just far enough to cover the thread. Remove the coarse thread and dip the tips about 1 inch in the violet dye. Unfold and, holding the outer edges together, dip them $1-1\frac{1}{2}$ inches in the violet dye.

XII:2 Flower cross pattern

Fold and tie as in the two-dye instructions (a) to (f) on page 80. Foundation dye in turquoise. Dip the five peaks in the middle in the violet dye far enough to cover the clothespins completely. Keep these peaks gathered together. Remove the middle clothespins so that only the six clothespins at each side are left. Dip each of the six folded sections of the one wing of the triangle separately in the violet dye so that the clothespins are covered, keeping the material gathered. Remove the pegs and, without unfolding the material, dye the same sections in a similar fashion in the yellow dye. Follow the same procedure with the six pleated sections from the other wing of the triangle. Finally, unfold the material and dip the outer edges to a depth of $1-1\frac{1}{2}$ inches in the violet dye, holding the material gathered together.

XII:3 Peasant flower pattern

Fold and tie as in the two-dye instructions (a) to (g) on page 81. Foundation dye in turquoise. Dip the M hold along the 10 inch side in the violet dye deep enough to cover the clothespin. Dip the M hold on the $17\frac{1}{2}$ inch side similarly in the violet dye. Remove both clothespins on the $17\frac{1}{2}$ inch side and dip the material to the same depth as before but this time in the yellow dye. Remove the clothespin by the M hold on the 10 inch side and dip in the yellow dye to the same depth as in the violet dye. Then dip each of the tips bound with coarse thread separately in the violet dye. Remove the thread and again dip in the violet dye, giving the *tip* of the tips a little extra dyeing time. Unfold the material and refold in three concertina pleats (each half-pleat measuring $3\frac{3}{4}$ inches) but working in the opposite direction. Again make two M holds in the $17\frac{1}{2}$ inch side and clip on clothespins as before. Finally, dip the two M hold sections first in the violet dye then in the yellow dye.

XII:4 Flowering creeper pattern

Fold and tie as in the two-dye instructions (a) to (d) on page 82. Foundation dye in turquoise. Dip the tip in the violet dye until the string tie is $\frac{1}{2}$ inch under the dye. Remove the tie and again dip in the violet dye, giving the outermost edges a little extra dyeing time. Then dip each of the five pinned M holds separately in the violet dye to a depth of $1\frac{1}{2}$ inches, holding the material in gathers. Remove one of the clothespins but retain the M hold and dip the tip in the yellow dye just far enough to cover the white dots. Proceed similarly with the four remaining M holds. Unfold and then refold in five concertina pleats (each half-pleat measuring $4\frac{1}{2}$ inches) working in the opposite direction. Make each separate pleat into an M hold and clip on five clothespins as before. Finally, dip the concertina pleats with the M holds in the dye as before, first in the violet, then in the yellow dye. See illustration on page 44.

XIII S-shape designs
XIII:1 River pattern
Fold and tie as in the two-dye instructions (a) to (f) on page 84.
Foundation dye in turquoise. Bind on extra isolating string ties at
the four additional points as described in (g) on page 84 and
remove the two end ties made before the first dyeing. Hold the
fabric by the ends and dip in the violet dye until the dye is $\frac{1}{2}$ inch
above the white stripes. Remove the three string ties in the central
section and dip the middle section in the yellow dye so that the
green central stripes are completely covered. Finally, dip the
short ends in the violet dye to a depth of 2 inches, holding the
material folded in two with the right side on the outside and
gathered together.

XIII:2 Star pattern
Fold and tie as in the two-dye instructions (a) to (f) on page 84.
Foundation dye in turquoise. Remove the three clothespins on
each of the outer edges so that only the middle clothespin
remains. Clip on an additional seven clothespins at X. Hold the
fabric by the ends and dip the central section in the violet dye
until the topmost white dots are just covered. Remove the central
clothespin which was placed in position before the foundation
dyeing. Altogether there should now be seven clothespins. Dip
the middle section to a depth of 3 inches in the yellow dye, holding
the material nearest the nearest side clothespins in gathers.
Finally, dip the short sides about 2 inches in the violet dye, keeping
the material folded in half with the right side on the outside and
gathered.

XIII:3 Double S pattern
Fold and tie as in the two-dye instructions on page 85. Untold
and refold in half horizontally with the right side outside (the
material will then measure $17\frac{1}{2} \times 11\frac{1}{2}$ inches). Fold the material
fan-fashion so that the narrowest end coincides with the center
fold. Gather together the fan in the center and dip the top to a
depth of 5–6 inches in yellow dye, giving a little extra dyeing time
to the tip. Finally, dip the short ends about 2 inches in the violet
dye, holding the material folded in half with the right side on the
outside and gathered.

XIII:4 Javanese curves
Fold and tie as in the two-dye instructions (a) to (f) on page 85.
Foundation dye in turquoise. Clip on an extra seven clothespins at
X as described in XIII:2 (g) on page 84. Dip all the edges on which
clothespins are clipped about $\frac{1}{4}$ inch in the violet dye holding the
material in concertina pleats. Remove the center clothespin first
positioned and dip the central section to a depth of 4–$4\frac{1}{2}$ inches in
the yellow dye. Remove the clothespins and unfold the material.
Once more centrally fold the material with the same side on the
outside following XIII:1, diagram (a) on page 83. Pleat both sides
of the material fan-fashion working in the opposite direction, that
is, so that the slanting line which marks the first pleat runs from
6 inches down on the left-hand side to 1 inch down on the right-
hand side. Clothespins are again used as isolating agents. Now
dip all the pinned edges to a depth of about $\frac{1}{4}$ inch in the violet dye

Shape tie-dyeing on pastel material. The undyed cloth shows how the pattern of the kerchief was obtained by following the penciled outline. The shapes (marbles, buttons and nuts) were twisted up in the material and secured with rubber bands.

while holding the material in concertina pleats. Remove the middle clothespin first positioned and dip the middle section to a depth of 4—4½ inches in the yellow dye. Finally, dip the short sides about 2 inches in the violet dye, holding the material folded in half with the right side on the outside and gathered.

Other tie-dyeing techniques

So far the book has concentrated on the basic methods of folding, tying and dyeing. These, as we have shown, provide a wide variety of designs and a basis for individual tie-dye work, but once you have mastered them you may wish to try your hand at the more specialized techniques outlined in the following section. They are not difficult to execute and most may be used either separately or in conjunction with other methods. Do not be afraid to experiment: with a touch of imagination these variations on the tie-dye theme will add greatly to the scope—and to the enjoyment—of your work.

Knot batik

This is the making of a tie-dye pattern by tying knots in the material itself rather than binding it with an isolating agent. The technique requires a fine material. Work lightheartedly and with gay abandon. First soak the material, then, to make a more symmetrical pattern, fold it in half. Lightly fold or pleat it, vertically or even diagonally, and make it up into a long strip. Tie a knot in the center and at each side of the center. Tie the ends into one or more knots. After the foundation dye the whole strip may be dipped in a contrast dye —or alternatively the center may be dipped in one color and the two ends in another slightly different color. It is, however, usually better not to use too strong a color but instead to repeat the process with the material folded and tied the other way round—with suitable variations in the knotting and coloring. A specimen of advanced knot batik is illustrated on page 103, the symmetry of patterning and the fine-drawn, clear-cut designs have been achieved by:

(i) Folding the wetted material in half lengthwise to allow even penetration of the dye.
(ii) Making sure the material is folded and not puckered—this gives a more clearly emphasized design.
(iii) Keeping the material smooth and flat wherever it is not folded.
(iv) Tying the knots symmetrically and mirror-fashion—that is, left-hand side knots are tied as mirror images of the right hand-side knots. When completed the fabric shows this same regular mirrored reflection.

Roll batik

This is quite simply the rolling up of strips of foam rubber in material before dyeing it. No complicated folding is required. The rubber strip should be no thicker than 1 ×1 inch for small lengths of material and correspondingly thicker for longer lengths. For best results do not use too coarse a material or too many thicknesses of it.

To use this method successfully first place a strip of foam rubber as described along each of the short sides of the material and roll them up in the material, working toward the middle until the two rolls meet. Reverse the material and roll up both short ends to meet the middle. Secure with rubber bands placed a little way in from the edges. Dip the whole fabric in a foundation bath then, if you wish, dip the ends in a contrast dye up to $\frac{1}{2}$ inch from the edge. After unfolding, the material may be pleated along its length and from $1\frac{1}{2}$–2 inches of the edges dipped in a contrast dye. As the foam rubber absorbs the dye and also keeps the material from being compressed a more even dyeing is obtained.

This technique may be varied. For instance, try placing the foam-rubber strips lengthwise along the long sides, with the material rolled up toward the middle; or fold each strip concertina-fashion, and secure it with a rubber band around each; or instead of *strips* of foam rubber use little cushions of it and roll them up in each corner.

Gathered batik
Striped gathers
Size of material $17\frac{1}{2} \times 35$ inches
(a) Soak the material. Fold the long side in half, then fold in half again. (b) Unfold and mark the resulting three creases with a pencil. (c) Gather the material along the central line, double it over and secure with a rubber band $\frac{1}{2}$ inch from the top. Repeat this process with the remaining two creases and also along the short sides. (d) Hold the material by means of the three bunches of gathers secured by the rubber bands and dip the four outer corners up to two-thirds of their length. Rinse, but still keep the material gathered together. Hold the material by the tips of the four corners. Remove the rubber bands. Dip up to two-thirds of the material in another contrast dye.

Checkered gathers
Size of material 17×34 inches
(a) Soak the material. Fold in half lengthwise. (b) Fold into a square measuring $8\frac{1}{2} \times 8\frac{1}{2}$ inches. Fold this into a triangle and press down firmly. (c) Unfold the material until it is once again folded double lengthwise. Mark in the zigzag crease so produced with a pencil. (d) Gather together the material all along the zigzag line. Straighten out the five corners thus obtained. (e) Hold firmly by the gathers and dip the whole work in a contrast dye. (f) Unfold until it is a square once again, then fold into a triangle but this time across the other diagonal so that when opened up as before the new zigzag line crosses over the first one. Gather up the material along this zigzag line as before. Dip the material again in contrast dye in the same way as before.

Semicircular gathers
Size of material 25×20 inches
(a) Soak the material. (b) Fold it in half to measure $12\frac{1}{2} \times 20$ inches. Mark in a penciled cross running from corner to corner. Using both hands at the same time gather the material together along

Advanced knot batik showing a systematic working out of the design.

the penciled lines beginning from the short side. (*c*) Place a rubber band over each of the two bunches of gatherings. (*d*) Dye the whole material in one color then dip the center in a contrast dye, first from the one side, then from the other. Remove the rubber bands and repeat the contrast dyeing. Then dip the gathered outer edges in a contrast dye to a depth of 2 inches.

Tack tie-dyeing

Gathers are usually made with the fingers along a penciled line. This gives very pleasing, lively results, but the patterns thus obtained do tend to be somewhat irregular. To make a more regular gathered design sew tacking stitches along the marked line and draw the material up as with a draw string, rearranging the gathers as evenly as possible. These gathers are kept in position by binding the thread around firmly several times and tying string around the whole to keep it in place. The thread used must obviously be strong and preferably white so that there is no risk of it running. Note: do not knot both ends of the thread; this makes needless untying work later.

The use of double tacking can be effective. This is done by folding the material in two along the marked-out line and then sewing fairly small tacking stitches through both layers of material a fraction in from the edge.

Tack tie-dyeing is particularly useful for marking wavy or zigzag borders but the isolating ties must, in this case, be very fine. This applies also to the production of geometrical figures. Such figures should be fairly large and not too complex; double tacking will make the task easier. A fresh thread will be needed for each new angle but the threads should not be "drawn" until the whole of the design has been tacked. It is important to pull the threads as strongly as possible and then to fasten them securely to ensure that the dye does not penetrate. The tacked design should preferably be dyed in some pale or pastel color. Note: it is hardly worth while using this method to make small irregular figures as the subsequent removal of the threads is both lengthy and tedious and the design may well turn out fuzzy and insignificant.

Spontaneous tie-dyeing

To most people "spontaneous art" suggests a canvas over which color has been splashed in a glorious free-for-all of the imagination with no definite motif, theme or subject. The same approach may be used in tie-dyeing, but the technique itself guides, in some degree, the result produced. The form of this craft does, by its nature, provide unlimited scope for the imagination, but if the end-result is to be attractive some forethought is essential. Start with a simple project which will give some idea of the possibilities of this particular form of textile art. If you have *no* idea of the ultimate shape of your work it may be a good idea to build up your design gradually. For instance, begin by dyeing a handful of the material some light color. Spread out the whole fabric and study it carefully before proceeding further. Maybe a pattern of rays would look well in one corner (fan-folding) or a central cluster of stars (circular gathering). Possibly a few narrow lines, or broader stripes, or a branching network is called for. Should these start and end nowhere in particular? Should the middle section be the broadest part of the design (expanding concertina pleating)? The possibilities are endless.

Once the project starts to take shape keep a hot iron and layers of newspaper handy, so that the result can be judged dry, (but do not forget to wet the material again before doing any further work on it). Sometimes it may be possible, with due caution, to apply a little color here and there. Dip a hard bristled paint-brush in the dye, hold it some 5–15 inches above the material at a point where spattering would not come amiss, then stroke the bristles with the index finger. Smaller areas can also be colored by dipping foam-rubber pieces in the dye and dripping them on to suitable patches. Do not forget that too gaudy colors can be toned down by a skillful use of shading.

It is useful to have a number of dyes available in quite small but concentrated amounts—$\frac{1}{2}$ pint is enough for quite a number of dyeings. Be sure to rinse carefully between each dyeing operation to avoid any risk of mixing the dyes.

Tie-dyeing combined with wax batik

For this, a stencil is used for the fine detail and the broad general design is printed on. Steep a paint-brush in melted wax and delineate the areas to be isolated. Dye as in ordinary tie-dyeing. The gathering of the material so characteristic of wax batik produces an attractive *craquelure* effect on the waxed areas. The fabric is usually dyed several times and shading can be used to effect. One advantage of the method is that the waxing is only carried out the first time although three or four colors can be introduced. The fine veining effects produced in tie-dyeing give the design its own very individual character. Aim to achieve a happy balance between the waxed pattern and the tie-dyed design. See illustration below.

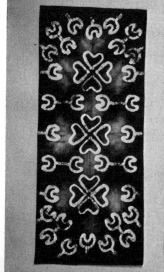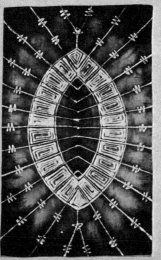

A printing-block design based on the creases made following cross pattern instructions in the basic section (the blocks are made of pipe-cleaners). A tjanting design based on creases made by folding according to instructions for the double fan in the basic design section.

Tie-dyeing combined with hand-printing

To many people a mixture of styles is anathema. If the end-result is pleasing, however, why should textile crafts not be combined? If you enjoy hand-printing then why not execute some mono-tone contrast dyeing and use this as a background for the printing—in this way the background has more life and can be made to adapt more closely to the design and the measurements used. Or, bolder still, why not use several colors in the tie-dyed background.

The real skill of this will lie in choosing a tie-dye pattern that will marry well with the hand-printed design. Tie-dye work executed in pastel colors can be combined equally well with embroidery. An embroidered scroll, can, for instance, be used to bring out the essence of an otherwise diffused design. An effective and unusual evening dress could well be made from tie-dyed satin embroidered with pearls or sequins.

Shape tie-dyeing

Collect together a number of odds and ends which will serve as "shapes." If these are irregular in size and contour then arrange them on the fabric in a random fashion. Wrap each one separately in the material. This will make a "neck" around which a rubber band, or string, is tightly fastened. If the shapes are all similar then try arranging them in a regular design marked out in pencil beforehand. The following make roughly circular outlines: peas, buttons, pebbles, corks, fir-cones, wine-glasses, marbles, bottle-tops.

To make a symmetrical design outline one-half of it in charcoal then fold the material and the charcoal design will rub off on to the other side giving the rest of the pattern. Before starting to draw the pattern it is a good idea to fold the material as you intend to fold it then unfold it and draw the pattern taking into account the creases produced by the folds. After the foundation dyeing remove the shapes, refold the material in the same design and dip it in a contrast dye.

Cushions are still needed in the homes of today and a "spontaneous" design meets the purpose admirably.

Embroidery enthusiasts may, as here, embellish the design with delicate needlework.

Tack tie-dyeing is the best method of producing a design based on regularly spaced gathers.

This small cloth in roll batik is a typical example showing the charming feathery design so characteristic of this particular technique.

Index